I0791379

Other books by the same author, to include pen names

Fiction
Antipodes 10, by John Pascal
Antipodes 20, by John Pascal
The Imposture & Other Tales; Thirty Short Stories, by John Pascal
The Shaggy Dog and Other Stories, by John Pascal
The Dartist, by John Pascal
Travels With My Ass, by John Pascal
The Resurrection of Charles Witchway, by John Pascal

Non-Fiction
Polwar: The Politicization of Armed Forces, by Pascal R. Politano
A Sharp Seasoning of Truth: A Comprehensive Commentary in the Pursuit of Genuine National Security, by Pascal R. Politano
Refractions, by Pascal R. Politano
Solo: A Guide for Men Whose Fate is Not to Endure the Raptures of Marriage, by Atticus Grammaticus
The Modern Day Gentleman and Other Essays, by Atticus Grammaticus

Poetry
The Man in the Moon, by Pascal R. Politano
Painting the Lily, by Pascal R. Politano
A Poet's Choice, by Pascal R. Politano

A Sharper Seasoning of Truth;

An Indictment of our Current System of Capitalist Democracy

Pascal R. Politano

authorHOUSE

AuthorHouse™
1663 Liberty Drive
Bloomington, IN 47403
www.authorhouse.com
Phone: 833-262-8899

Published by AuthorHouse 10/17/2022

ISBN: 978-1-6655-7115-9 (sc)
ISBN: 978-1-6655-7114-2 (e)

Library of Congress Control Number: 2022917351

Print information available on the last page.

Any people depicted in stock imagery provided by Getty Images are models, and such images are being used for illustrative purposes only.
Certain stock imagery © Getty Images.

This book is printed on acid-free paper.

The Worship of Mammon by Evelyn De Morgan

This book is dedicated to the nineteen small children and two of their teachers who were slaughtered at the Robb Elementary School at Uvalde, Texas on the 24th of May, 2022, while 396 law enforcement officers from at least three different agencies, armed and armored, stood by ineffectually, pusillanimously for well more than an hour, while one teenaged murderer continued to kill his helpless victims. To those craven cowards who responded to the ghastly emergency must be added those higher officials, to include the Governor of Texas, who continue to deceive, mislead, and blatantly lie to the public to avoid being accountable, along with those lily-livered responders. Lying now is competing successfully with Truth in this country, and "If You Did It, Deny It" has become a national motto.

FOREWORD

Customarily, the preface or foreword to a larger work is a bit of prose to give the reader some idea of what will be found in the main text in more detailed exposition. In its essence this book is about Justice and its indispensable attendant, Truth, both of which have become almost eclipsed in our sociopolitical cosmos.

Too many Americans tend to seek comfort, and more especially, entertainment, everywhere, however ominous the news, both domestic and foreign, may be. Unfortunately, there are times in our mixed lives when happiness and reality don't coincide. There was a time when a person who lived in New England and hated the cold winters could move to Florida, or in an obverse situation some Floridian who preferred the change of seasons. Now, with the nemesis of climate change looming over us, for which we have only ourselves to blame, within the foreseeable future not merely those geographical malcontents, but no one, anywhere, will be able to seek a place of refuge just to stay alive.

This book is not intended to entertain you, rather, its intent is to inform you of the precarious state of our union both here and abroad. I can only advise anyone who may have acquired a copy of this work seeking to be entertained to give it to a more serious reader. Still, I have tried to insert a few lines of comic relief here and there to help maintain your interest, however ironically they may have been intended. On the more serious side, I'll give you a few examples of issues and problems that are discussed more fully in the text.

Racism is as prevalent as it has been in the past although it is not so arrant or openly displayed as it was in those days of "Jim Crow." This, as in the matter of LGBTQ, is in major part due to our behavioral guru that we call political correctness. In the latter case the appearance of the Monkey Pox virus with its incidence of ninety-seven percent of its cases among homosexuals did not help the cause of those who advocate for same-sex marriage. Gun control has become a meaningless misnomer; there *is* no gun control. There is the fact that 50,000 children failed to appear for the first day of school in the Los Angeles area. This undoubtedly was due to some extent to the COVID-19 pandemic, and to the teaching of race relations, LGBTQ issues and gender ideology, but what percentage of those children and their parents were in fear of those mass shootings in schools that are occurring with ever increasing frequency? Perhaps such truancy will alleviate the nationwide shortage of teachers, due in part to the inequitable scale of wages they receive for so important an occupation, as well as their fear of those mass murders in which a number of teachers also have been killed or wounded. Meanwhile a number of States are considering arming their teachers. What can we expect next? As one gallows humorist suggested a few years ago: Why don't we just issue a loaded pistol to each student as he or she gets on the school bus every morning?*

Of political interest also is the fact that in the Midterm primaries twenty-one of thirty-six candidates for Governor

---

* As well as a serious shortage of teachers in our public schools, we also are experiencing a significant shortage of school bus drivers.

and eleven State Secretaries, one of whose primary duties is the supervision of elections in his or her State, and all of them Republicans, and all of whom are 2020 Presidential election deniers (believe Trump won), won their primaries. That's portentous news apropos of the 2024 Presidential election, if Trump isn't indicted, tried, and convicted of at least one criminal act and is imprisoned somewhere. If he still is a free man in 2024 we can blame our judicial system which is in total disarray and has become more political than juridical. As I've said in the dedication of this book, lying now is competing successfully with truth in this country and IF You Did It, Deny It has become a national motto.

In the prescient advice that he gave the people of this newly freed Republic, George Washington, in his Farewell Address (17 September, 1796) said this:

> The nation which indulges toward another habitual hatred or a habitual fondness…is a slave to its animosity or to its affection, either of which is sufficient to lead it astray. Sympathy for the favorite facilitating the illusion of a common interest, in cases where no real common interest exists, and infusing into one of the enmities of the other, betrays the former into a participation in the quarrels and wars of the latter, without adequate inducement or justification. It leads also to…jealousy, ill will, and a disposition to retaliate, in the parties from whom equal privileges are withheld. And it gives to ambitious, corrupted or deluded citizens (who devote themselves to the favorite Nation) facility to betray or sacrifice the

interests of their own country…Real Patriots, who
may resist the intrigues of the favorite, are liable
to become suspected and odious while its tools
and dupes usurp the applause and confidence of
the people and surrender their interests.

Now think of Israel, our "greatest ally in the Middle
East" which, since its questionable establishment three-
quarters of a century ago, has permitted us to have only
the pro forma detachment of U.S. Marine Corps guards at
our embassy in Jerusalem as our only armed force in their
entire country.

Our complete disregard of Justice for all the peoples of
the Middle East, driven by motives of power and avarice
and blatant xenophobia can in some ways be compared to
the havoc caused by the Christian Crusades of the 11th,
12th, and 13th centuries to win The Holy Land from the
Muslims. Can you not see that the turmoil in the Middle
East is largely of our own making? And we can assassinate
as many of those Muslim leaders, good or bad, that we
can boast about; there will always be another waiting in
the wings to replace him, if not immediately, then not
much later.

And finally there is this. Since the Constitution
prohibits honors, to include the bestowing of titles* and
other distinctions, we have evolved our own class system,
based upon wealth. That pleases the "upper class" rich, but

---

* Although Article III, Section 9 of the Constitution provides for the
bestowal of noble titles with the consent of of Congress, there have been only
two such titles given: one to the late former President Ronald Reagan and
to former President George W. Bush, both knighthoods.

leaves "the great unwashed" dying of old age but unable to retire, bagging groceries or flipping hamburgers in fast food chains that are killing people with diseases worsened or caused by our epidemic of obesity, and unable to afford the medications they need to keep them alive longer; dying from diseases such as diabetes or cardiovascular disorders. The legislation President Biden just managed to get through Congress apropos of Government negotiation of prices with the pharmaceutical companies won't take effect for several more years. Meanwhile, people are being made homeless by the ravages caused by climate change, and it is already too late to avoid or even mitigate the catastrophe that will bring the end of all life as we know it on this planet without some form of Divine Intervention. As to that last dismal note, even those of you who may be rigorously religious may ask yourselves if we humans are truly worthy of redemption and salvation.

1

This work, with all deference to Sam. Johnson and his Eighteenth Century periodical *The Rambler*, will be a ramble of its own kind, that is, a more comprehensive but not rigorously cohesive summary of my writings during the COVID-19 pandemic.*

Unless we were engaged in a fully-fledged war, the state of our Union could not be in greater jeopardy. In reality, it is more a matter of the state of the populace within it. Once the Rocky Mountains were often referred to as The Great Divide; today that title would be more fitting, if not so grandiloquent, to describe the 330 million people who like to call themselves Americans. How did this happen? More to the point, *why* did this happen? What has split this country virtually in two?

Of course we must consider that "how" of matters as they developed: it's a matter of prime importance. But it is the "why" whose answer is of even more seriousness and relevance to the quandary in which we now find ourselves. At this point, President Biden may well be in his bed, or even under it, in a darkened room clutching that hockey stick he has so valiantly been trying to shoot pool with. After being in office little more than a year and a half it is more than likely that he has come to the realization that despite what we may hear from those benighted Constitutional "Originalists," our existing system of capitalist democracy has failed to a crucial extent and may be on the verge of a complete breakdown. If there is to be any hope for us at all it could begin by

---

* See *As Darkness Falls: From Notes Taken During the Great Pandemic, 2020-2021,* by the same author.

holding a Constitutional Convention. As I have said before, our Constitution is not Holy Writ; no matter how we may revere it, it is simply a publication of laws, organization and doctrine laid down by men for the governance of the people of this country, ratified 231 years ago.

Why, at the outset, did I say that the state of the populace, meaning its attitudes and dispositions, was a major factor in the state of our sociopolitical disarray? Today and for many years past, we have been suffocated with news, "entertainment" of every kind to include sports, movies, TV series, and "reality" shows, all on multitudinous channels, and more recently an avalanche of social media with its opinions and commentaries (based on fact or pure fiction), and not least advertising, commercials on TV, most of which are as garish, tiresome, and unsightly as the hundreds of thousands of billboards and other commercial signs that clutter our roadsides and urban areas—painted, in neon lights, electromechanical— suffocatingly. One big jolly ride on that social rollercoaster we like to think of as "normalcy". But what are we expected to believe? What is important to our very existence? What should we be thinking about and really be interested in? In all this delusive atmosphere of lighthearted apathy that can be so destructive to our true and best interests, what can the legitimate news outlets, however good and even altruistic their intentions may be, do about it? Remember that their sponsors are ever present. And there we have a dilemma, or at least a great irony in our system of capitalist democracy.

Despite the Federal law which prohibits the use of propaganda within our own country we literally are drowning in it. If psywar (now psyop, to include psywar) and commercial advertising are not sisters they are at the very least first cousins. The only significant difference lies in their objectives: the former is employed in hot or cold war, or in relatively peaceful times to further what we consider to be our best interests; the latter, more simply stated, is profit. But the techniques are essentially identical: target analysis, campaign planning, vulnerabilities and susceptibilities, attitudes and behavior, objective(s), classification of sources—white, grey, or black— i.e., revealed, uncertain, unrevealed. In short, an experienced former psyoperator shouldn't have any problem upon retirement of moving through that swinging door and getting a position at one of those advertising agencies on Madison Avenue.

So when the top news concerning Britney Spears' court case had subsided, and while the Russians were massing troops on the Ukrainian border, and the COVID-19 pandemic was surging again, we had, leading the news on CNN the riveting report that William Shatner (Captain Kirk of *Star Trek* fame) was preparing to visit "space" in what appeared to be a huge erected human phallus. Seemingly of secondary importance were matters that I find difficult to categorize since they all were of cardinal importance, such as those I mentioned above.

The pandemic moves toward its third year, with the death toll over one million and rising steadily. Gun violence and the opiate epidemic continue unabated and are on the rise across the nation. Democrats and Republicans remain at daggers drawn, with intramural squabbling between progressive and moderate factions within the Democrats' ranks. The inequitable distribution of wealth continues as the rich have gained a trillion dollars thus far during the pandemic. Our judicial system, to include the Supreme

Court, is in total disarray. As only one example, all Federal Judges should not be appointed for life terms. In the area of foreign affairs, we have little justification to claim that we are the world's leaders in democracy anymore since it has become clear that we are unable to solve our own domestic problems. Racism in America is as prevalent as ever and the efforts to eradicate it are only making matters worse. As to that climate conference in Glasgow, how could anything useful have been accomplished absent the two world leaders in pollution, China and Russia? In any case, as to global warming, it's too late to avoid what seems inevitable; we have passed the "tipping point" and can expect Nature's wrath to continue and worsen because of man's avarice and apathy, until the cataclysmic extinction of all life as we know it on this planet. And as France's President Macron told our Congress a few years ago. "There is no planet 'B'." Then there is the supply chain, with all those ships waiting offshore and those cargo containers piling up at U.S. ports waiting for transport to their destinations and contributing to the alarming rise in inflation. I'll leave it to you to have read this depressing list of our problems to decide what the priority of trying to solve them should be, problems that President Biden must face every day when he arises after a restless and even a sleepless night. Added to all this, the growing crisis in eastern Europe is portentously ominous, and although I haven't mentioned immigration issues, which though not much in the news presently, are worse than ever but seem to be all but forgotten amid the storm of other crises we face. Meanwhile, Governor Abbott of Texas has bussed 9,000 immigrants from South and Central America to New York City and Washington, D.C. But let us continue to ramble a little further in this maze of failing democracy.

In that bittersweet period of our history during the early 1960s, after our clumsy, failed attempt to invade Cuba and rid it of Fidel Castro and his communists, then that brief halcyon period of "Camelot at the White House," the nearly cataclysmic Cuban missile crisis, and the still mysterious assassination of President Kennedy, I was in the Far East. While there I met two Britishers, one a Foreign Office functionary, the other a correspondent for the BBC.* While we were having a drink together I noticed that both men spoke in what some call "the gentle voice," others "the Oxford sound." Obviously they were, in England's social structure, of the upper middle class. After chatting a bit desultorily for a while, the recent and still much debated JFK assassination came up. The BBC man was convinced that the actual cause of Kennedy's killing was an internal political one to nullify Kennedy's disinclination to become involved in a war with the Vietnamese communists. He was adamant about the matter, and to lighten or at least divert the conversation I asked his companion what he thought of the fact that the Kennedy family had on a number of occasions been referred to as one of America's "royal families." At first the other looked slightly dazed, then he began to look at me as if my clothes didn't fit, or that I had gone to the wrong school. I turned back to the journalist, who was staring at me as if I were something nasty he had just scraped off his shoe. But moments later we were drinking toasts and laughing uproariously.

____

* If you watch the BBC news on our PBS channels, you'll get better and more factual information about what's going on in the rest of the world.

What is the purpose of this little anecdote, you may ask. It is simply this: if the United States has any class system at all it is based upon wealth, money. Everything, including even some of our myriad religious institutions, as has been proven, is driven by the great God Mammon in the acquisition of wealth. One could say that we are a latter-day, solid state version of Fritz Lang's 1927 film *Metropolis*, wherein the rich play above and the poor toil below, where they fruitlessly and piteously try to emulate and imitate the rich by living beyond their means. And I'm sure those two Brits I spoke of were aware of that old British adage: it takes 600 years to cultivate a proper English lawn; and it takes just as long to produce a proper English gentleman. Joe Kennedy, JFK's father and once U.S. Ambassador to Great Britain, added significantly to the pile left to his wife Rose by her father, "Honey Fitz" Fitzgerald of Boston notoriety. Papa Joe made his pile by running illicit booze from Canada into the U.S. during Prohibition while taking trips to the West Coast to bed Hollywood star Marion Davies, newspaper magnate William Randolph Hurst's sometime mistress, at Hurst's palatial residence of San Simeon. While he was filling his ambassadorial post at the Court of St. James his young son Jack, our future and unfortunate 35th President, was making everything but his bed in pre-war England. A generation later Jack and his brother Bobby (assassinated five years after his brother) enjoyed an arrangement similar to their father's with the Davies, by bedding Marylyn Monroe.

The brilliant young statesman and scholar Alexis De Tocqueville, on touring what then was our new Republic in the early nineteenth century, wrote this in his two-volume book *Democracy in America*: "I know of no country indeed, where the love of money has taken a stronger hold on the affections and where a profounder contempt is expressed for the theory of the permanent equality of property." There it is; nothing's changed, barring inflation. We fought a war to become a classless democracy, and all we have accomplished is to redefine the word "class." In Great Britain, that is in large part responsible for this outcome; a man can be as rich as Croesus, but if he owned a chain of tobacconists shops or even a score of coal mines he still would be referred to somewhat deprecatingly as "being in trade." Once again, you can't make a good pot out of poor clay, or a silk purse out of sow's ear, to cite just two American aphorisms.*

I have mentioned the fact that the wealthiest people in this country, in great part those on Wall Street, profited a trillion dollars last year. Those people, with their lawyers and accountants and with the tax code as it now reads managed to pay no taxes at all.† So what is all this wrangling about raising taxes on the rich? President Biden himself has claimed publicly that the fifty-five biggest companies in the nation paid no taxes at all in 2020. So if the rich paid no taxes at all why all this controversy over raising their taxes? Something added to nothing still is something. It can only be the fear of those who reject any change that would require a closer look at the existing rules and the loopholes that the big boys

---

* Or as the Germans would have it, more eloquently, *Aus so krümmen Holz, als woraus der Mensch gemacht ist, kann nichts ganz Gerades gezimmert warden*—out of the crooked timber of humanity no straight thing can ever be made.

† Since the advent of our becoming an independent Republic there were no Federal income taxes, except when they were twice levied by Congress during the Civil War. The 16th Amendment, proclaimed in 1913, empowered Congress to lay and collect taxes on incomes "from whatever source derived."

batten upon to escape paying their fair share. To list only two champions of the rich, both Democrats and who, incidentally, continue to stall Biden's efforts to achieve Senatorial approval of a just voting rights act as well as legislation of several other sensible laws: Senator Krysten Sinema of Arizona (mainly the big pharmaceutical houses, who already are getting rich beyond the dreams of avarice on the vaccines and other medicinal necessities to fight the pandemic), and fellow Democrat Senator Joe Mancin (who is heavily invested in the coal mines of his home State of West Virginia). Coal baron Mancin's is a double evil if we consider our greatest threat, that of climate change due to air pollution.

Keep in mind that during the continuing pandemic, while Main Street was in dire financial straits, on Wall Street the Dow Jones Index was setting new record highs. President Biden himself admitted during this pandemic, which may last indefinitely, that the one-tenth of one percent of the population who already possess ninety percent of its wealth have already gained one trillion dollars more in profits. Clearly, our version of a capitalist democracy isn't failing; it already has failed, and if we, the people, don't see that then we have failed also. Again, we need a Constitutional Convention, and by now it should be obvious that we need one desperately. If our representatives in Washington keep stonewalling, and President Biden continues to be relatively ineffectual in his efforts to "do the right thing," however well-meant they may be, and Wall Street continues to reign over Main Street, we're finished, provided climate change doesn't claim us all first. This is also assuming that we won't have to endure the agonies of another civil war in the interim, about which I'll say more later. Money, that great god Mammon too many of us revere, if it defines our class system, if we have any class system at all, has become a seminal factor in our increasing record of systemic failures. Time wasted, about which I have written but will have more to say, is another crucial factor in our decline.

2

Americans like games; any games. If many of our highly-touted more than 5000 colleges and "universities"* didn't have football or basketball teams they would have to curtail their enrollments, their academic programs, hiring of qualified "educators," or in some cases simply have to close their doors. Salaries for coaches in some schools are now in the millions annually, far exceeding those of their scholastic "colleagues." Where space is available spectators now number over 100,000 and with very few exceptions must pay for their tickets; and that is to say nothing of the game-happy alumni and other contributors of donations to the schools. College football no longer is the amateur sport it once was; today it is a kind of minor league professional business, with basketball perhaps coming in an octave lower on the financial scale.

For the purpose of what I have to say now let us consider sex, not to exclude that "bastard muse" pornography, as a game. We humans, who are pleased to say that we are the only species in the animal kingdom who have been endowed, somehow, with an intellect, must not ignore that multi-billion dollar enterprise of pornography. Relatively few people use that intellect to solve Chinese box puzzles, Rubik's Cube, or just to play Chess. That is not to say that those same people don't enjoy sex, they just aren't

---

* State colleges and universities in this country should be tuition free as they are in most other civilized nations. It would not be unreasonable to add that students should defray their other expenses such as room and board.

obsessed with it. As for the majority of Earthlings, since they do have an intellect of some kind, they could learn to read, or at least interpret the pictures in certain books and magazines. The books might include but not be limited to Alex Comfort's 1972 bestseller *The Joy of Sex*, Kinsey's (et. al.) *Sexual Behavior in the Human Male*, followed by that in the *Human Female*. The graphic magazines in newsstands and bookshops can speak for themselves.

After the primal demand of self-preservation, sex is an innate, cyclic urge among what many people refer to as the "lesser" or "lower" animals in order to ensure the continued propagation of their species.* Hunters in Africa will tell you that when a bull elephant is in "must" (the urge to enjoy the charms of a female of the species), he is the most dangerous animal one can confront. There may be a little foreplay among certain species, but not much, and only to induce the female to share in her own delights. Sex? assuredly, but with a serious, if inbred, underlying purpose that persists among those "lesser" species, while for too many of we humans it has devolved into a game.

Do not misunderstand me; our attempts to find ways of making sex more enjoyable, some would say perverted, are nothing new, they go back for millennia in recorded history: the Hindu Kamasutra, the winged phallic images of the Ancient Greeks, the sleazy Parisian street vendors of La Belle Epoch who surreptitiously offered to sell you "feelthy pictures," are only a few examples. At the other

---

* Except perhaps for a small fish whose name I can't remember, which is self-reliant in that it fertilizes its own eggs in the process of reproduction. There probably are some female readers out there who wish they had the same self-sufficiency.

end of the sexual spectrum there are those I call "sexual purists," who would describe those sexual adventurers as "sexual perverts." If they were acquainted with Shakespeare, they might invoke what he said about gilding refined gold or adding another hue to the rainbow. You would find such married couples in the Bible Belt, who pull down their shades on a weekend afternoon and go hand in hand silently upstairs to their bedroom.

Explicit sex is, as are its companions, drugs and violence, everywhere today, ably assisted by the many advances in modern technology. Many are the various enhancements man's ingenuity has employed: topless waitresses and go-go dancers,* pornography, live, or on film, to include pedophilic films on the internet, and those relatively rare but truly depraved "snuff films," and of course the raft of graphically explicit magazines. Then there are the myriad devices, or "toys" as some would call them: whips, chains, leather, vibrators and other vaginal stimulators. All that, but the ultimate result, in most cases, is essentially the same as that experienced by that virtuous and incorruptible couple in the Bible Belt: orgasm, climax. There is no way to achieve sexual exaltation beyond that. There was a popular song not too many years ago entitled "Is That All There Is?" and that sums it up, at least in its title. Truly, America has become a country of very sharp contrasts, not merely politically, but at its very roots, demographically.

---

* As a small boy I watched as a woman in a semi-public place afforded her breast to her hungry, squalling infant. I was shocked as I watched, and too embarrassed to tell anyone about it when I got home, although I may have mentioned the incident to my (male) friends later.

The American songbook contains another much older number by Cole Porter whose lyrics begin with, "In olden days a glimpse of stocking was shocking, as everyone knows, now anything goes…" And then, more recently and adding to the confusion, there was Tina Turner's brash and incisive interjection, "What's love got to do with it?" There was a time, mainly before the Great War, when brides wearing the traditional chaste white wedding gowns weren't the pro forma farce accepted without comment today. There were of course a number of exceptions, but few had been living and sleeping with the prospective groom for months or even years. In some societies there was practiced the ritual of throwing the bloodstained sheets out the window on the morning after the wedding for the edification of the small gathering below, when pre-marital sex may have been practiced but was not to be spoken of.

Today, I have it on the very best authority that children in this country begin engaging in sex, mainly fellatio, in elementary school. In one prominent, private, coeducational elementary school, that same source has alleged, the children evolved a "Rainbow Club," wherein drawings were held using varicolored slips of paper, and thus the boy who was to enjoy the ministrations of the girl who drew the same color as he was chosen. A quantum advance over the old "spin the bottle," wouldn't you say? What I've been speaking about has little or nothing to do with morality or religious strictures; rather, it has everything to do with today's literally epidemic depression, suicides, and feelings of inadequacy, disillusionment, and the frustrating unfulfillment among so many young people in this country, while their concupiscible appetites drive them on to seek the real joy of sex. Among the rites of passage, sex has given all it had to give, and still they ask, is that all there is? Hence, drug use, and its concomitant fatalities, has more than doubled in the last ten years, the number of mass shootings is setting new records almost daily, and suicide has become commonplace; among the armed forces veterans there now is a suicide every hour. If that continues we'll make it even easier for our enemies to beat us; we won't have enough troops to fight another war.

Meanwhile, the social internet continues setting standards, mainly physical, that most young people can't achieve and contradicting political correctness in its insistence on that ill-conceived presumption of "I'm okay, you're okay".* The pharmaceutical commercials on TV are hammering away in huckstering products with cryptic names that are touted to cure or at least to alleviate medical problems that many people don't even know they are the victims of. One of these advertisements tells us to use their product when we're constipated, so we won't feel as if we are passing a pineapple(!), or as P.G. Wodehouse would describe it, a "fretful porpentine." Another features the image of a malformed carrot to illustrate how the human penis appears when afflicted by Peyronie's Disease. Now there's good taste in advertising for you! However appalling the casualty list may be, as long as the market surveys and their "algorithms" reveal the vulnerabilities and susceptibilities

---

* In 1969 Thomas Harris published a book entitled *I'm Okay-You're Okay* and by 1972 over half a million copies had been sold. This book gave significant impetus to what some societal observers have called The Great Leveling Process, which sadly always works in a downward trend.

of the targeted audience, the acquisition of wealth will rule, with pornography as one of its handmaidens.

In beginning my discussion of sex as a game, I referred to pornography as a "bastard muse"; I think the term deserves some clarification. The title is not of my own invention, but was introduced at Yale University years ago by a visiting lecturer from Great Britain. This scholar claimed that in addition to the nine commonly accepted muses of Greek mythology there were now three more "bastard muses in the United States." Perhaps there was one more, but the three I remembered were enough to serve the purpose for the book I was writing, and I remembered those clearly; if there was a fourth I'd be willing to bet it was that humbug political correctness we have had to endure. The three were Propaganda, Pornography, and Sentimentality, all of which you will find adequately explored in the volume cited below.*

---

* For an expanded discussion of this subject see "The Bastard Muses" in *A Sharp Seasoning of Truth* by the same author.

3

B ut our ramble has taken us, however obliquely, to the matter of justice; let us go there, to the hallowed halls of American jurisprudence. In 2020 there were one million, three-hundred thousand practicing defense attorneys in the United States. If we were to add their adversaries, prosecutorial attorneys at all levels of governance, the number would be exponentially higher. Is it any wonder that we have become the most litigious country in the world? What has this led to? There have been too many cases in criminal trials, some would call it a trend, in which the accused is exonerated, but later, in a civil suit, the court finds for the plaintiff, usually the victim's family, and decrees that huge amounts, often in the millions, be paid them, with a full one-third of the total award going to the plaintiff's attorney(s) (standard practice). I can't argue the astonishing amounts that have been awarded; no right-thinking person could put any price on a murdered son or other family member, but I do see what my ancestors would call a *non sequitur* (it does not follow), a logical fallacy in the dichotomous judgement of two courts of law, one criminal and the other civil. If a person is found not guilty of murdering someone how can he be found presumably guilty in a civil action involving the same offense and thus made to pay damages for that offense? The O.J. Simpson trial in a criminal court and subsequent civil suit provide a classic example of this judicial paradox, but there have been a number of others since. There must be some provision or precedent in the laws that permits this, but it seems like double jeopardy to me, and another justification for that Constitutional Convention I keep clamoring for.

Since 1925, the Supreme Court has expanded the meaning of the Fourteenth Amendment so as to include the whole of the First Amendment and selected portions of the Fourth to Eighth Amendments of the Federal Bill of Rights. Thus States may not abridge the freedom of speech, press, religion, assembly or petition, make unreasonable searches and seizures, keep people of a different color or nationality off jury lists, use physical coercion or prolonged questioning to obtain confessions, require excessive bail, deny an accused person an opportunity to cross-examine a hostile witness, deny counsel to an accused person at any stage of police questioning or judicial proceedings, or unduly speed up or delay a trial. Along the way, in 1967 (with its Summer of Love), the Court declared unlawful the laws banning miscegenation, which existed in fifteen southern and border States. Now the Court has made abortion unlawful just a few days after making the carrying of concealed firearms in public places legal, using that tired and much misinterpreted Second Amendment as justification. The Supreme Court, with its Trump appointed majority, no longer is a juridical body, it is merely another political one. Dwell on what I've written for a few moments. *Now* do you think our Constitution should be amended and brought up to date?

There have been times so apt, so fitting to a situation that I've wished I could take credit for this trenchant description of it. Many years ago in a movie called *The Star Chamber*, whose theme was vigilantism at the highest level, one of the players (I think it was Hal Holbrook) in the rôle of a reputable but renegade judge, said, and I paraphrase, "Justice has been kidnapped and is being held hostage by our legal system." Elsewhere, I have written extensively about our systemically failed judicial branch of governance,* and I will have more to say on that subject later in this work.

The opiate (now opioid) endemic, thus far in the current year has taken more than 100,000 lives, more than the death toll due to gun violence and auto fatalities combined. The primary killers in drug deaths, Fentanyl, Methamphetamine, and Oxycontin (Oxycodone), continue to take their grisly toll while the Governments at both State and Federal level remain stalled in bureaucratic wrangling over gun and birth control, the economy, immigration laws, and not least, climate change.

This just in. A commercial flight that left Florida enroute to England with 129 passengers abroad had to return to its point of departure because a female passenger refused to don a mask, which is required on all commercial airlines now. The flight was cancelled and no other scheduled for the other compliant people aboard, frustrating their plans to visit friends and relatives abroad. Nothing was said about the disposition of the miscreant woman. Was she arrested or at least detained by the authorities? Will she

---

* See *A Sharp Seasoning of Truth: A Comprehensive Commentary in Pursuit of Genuine National Security*, by the same author. Because of his wife's political and financial connections, Clarence Thomas should resign from the SCOTUS or be impeached. If he left the court, Biden might be able to replace him with a democrat to help even the odds on certain decisions if the Chief Justice sided with the more liberal members, as later it was revealed he did, staunchly.

be held accountable with some penalty such as a fine or even imprisonment? Should the airlines install detention equipment; handcuffs, leg irons, and the like to control such transgressors of the law? There have been more than a hundred incidents involving unruly passengers thus far in 2022. Is anything being done to resolve such outrageous disregard for the law?

4

Meanwhile, with no more news of Captain Kirk and his giant erected phallus on the launch pad or other such vital astronomical news to convey, CNN is devoting its precious time to our earthbound astrophysicists who, with the aid of their new Webb telescope are again searching for life as we know it (a true alien might exist on methane gas, or even be invisible to our limited senses), searching for that nebulous "Planet B" President Macron spoke of. However, if such a planet exists it would never be available for our exodus if we make *this* planet uninhabitable; and if they did find it we wouldn't have the means to reach it with the crude systems of "space" travel we are limited to. And can you imagine the frustration and exasperation in their ranks if those star searchers had to conclude that the universe actually has no bounds, is infinite; something that would be incomprehensible to our five limited senses to even the most "brilliant" among them.*

Consider that Big Bang theory that we are told holds the answer to how the universe came into being. Anyone who is acquainted with the basics of metaphysics, mainly cosmology and ontology (the study of Being in this case) will tell you that especially in such a cataclysmic event there must be a *prime mover*; simply put, any demolitionist worthy of the name will tell you that there must be a detonator

---

* This would be analogous to someone groping about in the Library of Congress in total darkness seeking to find a book written in a language he cannot read, and that has been removed from the stacks already.

and a fuze to cause an explosion, unless he wants to kill himself. What or who was the prime mover that caused that megaexplosion? And no, I'm not qualified nor am I inclined to bring religion into this discussion, especially some theological manifestation of Divine Intervention. I do enjoin the reader, whatever his religious persuasion, and even those of you who may not have one, to give what I've said some profound thought. Think also what that new Webb telescope, that some say is 100 times more powerful than the existing Hubbell, has cost the taxpayer ten billion dollars (thus far). I could suggest that those scientists abandon their fruitless search and admit to us that one thing *is* clear: whatever fantasies they engage in, it's too late to save us from the effects of climate change. Instead of star gazing, they should have been working on that problem since the Reagan administration. Those star gazers need no longer search for black holes. We all, on this relatively tiny planet, that is our only refuge, have created our own "black hole," and are on the verge of descending into its ominous yet inexplicable, perhaps even infinite, depths. Unless that still unknown agent, or entity, or prime mover that caused that "big bang" out of somewhere, sometime, decides to give us another chance for our salvation. We cannot be so arrogant as to think we just came to be, no matter how fervently theologically safe we can be through Divine Intervention.

Now we are being visited by another medical mystery, this one with more earthly connections (I hope). When it first made its appearance among members of our Embassy staff in Havana, Cuba it was named simply the "Havana Syndrome" since nothing was known about it except its symptoms: headaches, disorientation, dizziness, vertigo, and other manifestations of a general malaise. Not much later similar indispositions were being reported from locations around the world in similar U.S. and other venues. More recently this enigmatic disorder was given a more definitive name: "Pulse Electromagnetic Energy," which doesn't take the average layman very far in understanding what it is anymore than Havana Syndrome, and that probably is due to the fact that the people who have been trying to discover its cause don't themselves know. Why not just call it Idiopathic Syndrome, Etiology Unknown?

But after that mysterious but I hope interesting digression there is a little more to say about telescopes. Development of the Hubbell telescope, the predecessor of the Webb, had a two-billion-dollar cost overrun due to incompatible data exchanges between U.S. scientists and their foreign colleagues, since our people were using the old English system of weights and measures while their counterparts abroad made those calculations and computations using the simpler, more modern metric system. As a result, appropriate corrections and adjustments had to be made on the Hubbell scope while it was in orbit around the Earth. Those repairs could not be done remotely, but only by human hands. If a similar problem were found to exist with the Webb scope any such task would be impossible since it will be orbiting not Earth but the sun, 92 million miles away and a little too hot for comfort. The United States still refuses to adopt the metric system while all other nations with the exception of Burma (Myanmar) and Liberia have been using it for decades. More confusion exists since our armed forces have adopted the metric system in a quasiofficial way, with the old English system still making its appearance here and there from time to time. For years, Americans traveling abroad complained about the fact that wherever they went, the shower baths, if they existed at all, had hand-held shower heads (to provide greater mobility when bathing). "Why do they have to put them on hoses when they should be fixed to the wall like we do?" I've been asked. The same people would also wonder why the toilet bowls were in a separate little room accompanied only by a small wash basin. Just recently I've seen a TV commercial advertising hand-held shower heads, as if they were a new advance. In the majority of foreign countries, mobile shower heads came in with showers. Can we hope for separate toilet facilities as we move closer to the more civilized countries of the world? Why don't we stop trying to lead the world for a little while and catch up with it first?

*   *   *

Here I think it would be helpful to insert a brief note to the reader.

When I began to write this treatise, Russia had occupied the Crimea, eviscerated Chechnia, and killed hundreds of innocent Syrians with chemical weapons in support of that nation's dictatorial regime under Assad, and had begun to move troops to its border with Ukraine. When I was well into playing the self-appointed *advocatus diaboli* (devil's advocate) in judging the sanity of the state of our Union, the Russians had invaded Ukraine and events began to move and develop rapidly. Eight years earlier, Russia had moved into the Donbas region of Ukraine where they were welcomed by their sympathizers there; but this is war, whatever President Putin chose to call it.* The situation changed so quickly that you may find parts of this work somewhat historical, others journalistic as if I were bringing you the latest news about the progress of the war. Nonetheless, despite an occasional lack in continuity, I hope you will find that the completed dissertation is interesting and informative, or at the very least digestible.

The remainder of this work therefore will be, not a patchwork quilt, but still more of a rambler than I had at its outset intended. I will try to maintain as much cohesiveness as is within my capability, and do what I can to avoid those shifts of scene and subject that can be distracting and even annoying to the reader. Necessarily, however, there may be a few disconcerting but unavoidable changes in place and time.

*   *   *

And so we go on and on, as if we were experiencing a false sense of normalcy. The ship of state continues to sail serenely along through these potentially disastrous icebergs

---

* And it is keeping Georgia and Moldova in a state of uneasiness about the outcome of Putin's "military operation" in Ukraine. It is my opinion that if the European Union had had the sense to broaden its NATO membership, eastern Europe would not find itself in the predicament they're in now. One thing is certain: Russia needs one more revolution to rid itself of totalitarianism of any kind after centuries of despotic rule. The Czarists, Soviets, and now the Putin Regime have differed in name only. I suggest they try some form of democratic socialism under a constitution that suits these modern times and the desperate need for global fraternity.

(and now there are many more to match the metaphor as the great ice fields continue to calve increasingly and cascade into the deepening mother sea) showing only their summits while their ominous and deadly bulks are ignored. TV programming remains largely unchanged, with its overwhelming, unremitting hawking of pharmaceuticals given oddly contrived names and with specious claims that they will help you live longer, think more clearly, and will improve conditions you never knew you were suffering from; that and some of the most fattening foods conceivable, purportedly attractively arranged and displayed, but which look as if they've already been eaten or were just so much garbage ready to be disposed of.* Then there are those recurrent TV commercials selling cars, cars, cars. One wonders why, if trillions of dollars are needed for financial relief, new automobile sales are doing so well, especially at a time when inflation is rising alarmingly and gasoline prices are leading its rise. Meanwhile, as I've mentioned elsewhere, a product called Colace, a stool softener, tells us it will prevent us from feeling as if we were excreting a porcupine or a pineapple.† Another boon for the dignity of mankind.

---

* It is a fact that Americans discard, dispose of, forty percent of all edible food available to them, while in some countries people literally are starving to death. Paradoxically, obesity has reached epidemic proportions, as is evidenced by the fact the chairs in any number of waiting rooms have doubled in width. Nine million people died of starvation throughout the world in 2021.

† Predictably, this was (and unfortunately will be) a "voice-over" commercial; that of a female, whose contract probably included a clause that she would not be seen in this coarse commercial. This would be especially likely if the female were good looking, in order to preserve the illusion that pretty girls only excrete orange sherbet in little cellophane bags.

I see Alexis De Tocqueville smiling and nodding in his grave, while the great god Mammon settles himself more comfortably on his red, white, and blue throne.

Having given as the reason for my brief apologia the Ukrainian fracas, to include a little recent history as well as current events, seems appropriate here. In February of 2022, Russian troops took up positions along the entire Russo-Ukrainian border. At that time, 14,000 lives had already been taken since 2014 when the Russians made their first incursion into Ukraine's Donbas region, which is populated in great part by Russian sympathizers. With Ukraine virtually surrounded, in addition to the "lethal aid" the U.S. had been sending the Ukrainians, 8500 of our troops were placed on alert and units of the 82nd Airborne Division left for Eastern Europe. Aside from untold numbers of Russian soldiers wearing Ukrainian uniforms who were already "in country," the Russians now had almost 200,000 troops encircling Ukraine and in Belarus, its ally. Given those odds, depending on what NATO would do, the general consensus was that the Russians should be in the capital, Kyiv, a week after they crossed the border. In addition, to all this the Russians had positioned assault ships off Ukraine's Black Sea Coast.

In late February 2022, President Putin gave a one-hour speech to an international audience. When he had outlined his plans to "reclaim" those regions in southeastern Ukraine where, he asserted, the inhabitants wished to be repatriated to mother Russia, he went on to allege that other countries on Russia's western border declared their independence too precipitately after the fall of the Soviet Union and should have remained under the aegis of Russia. He waxed almost rhapsodic as he referred to "the Russian Empire" several times. Putin had been a relatively minor official in the Soviet intelligence service, an *apparatchik* blindly devoted to his superiors and his organization. Still, if we've had a paranoidal, narcissistic, sociopath in the White House, why shouldn't the Russians have a megalomaniac in the Kremlin? Belarus already is in Putin's game bag; Kazakhstan has welcomed the Russians who came to their assistance in quelling protests there; Finland, which is not a member of NATO and trying to stay neutral could become a victim of Putin's overarching schemes of territorial acquisition; even peace loving Sweden now is considering joining NATO.

Peace loving Sweden, that hasn't been at war for hundreds of years, and Finland, with its 800-mile border with Russia, are drawing closer to joining NATO, and with the outrage that continues in Ukraine, I hardly think they will be denied membership. President Putin is acutely aware of that Article Five in the NATO charter (war with one means war with all), and if that union were to become a reality it is just possible that the Russians might be willing to end the butchery in Ukraine through negotiation, if that is still at all possible. With almost all of the world's opprobrium already heaped upon his head, Putin, if he sees he cannot achieve some kind of victory in Ukraine, and if he still is rational enough to realize that if he loses his fearful grip on the Russian populace, he may someday have to face justice before the International Criminal Court, one can only hope he may take another way out, as did Hitler in May, 1945, when the Russians were entering Berlin.

Sweden's steel is prized throughout the world, and has been since a millennium or more ago when her process for converting iron into steel somehow reached as far as Damascus, making that city, which was then in Persia, renowned for its highly-prized swords throughout the Arab Crescent. I am pleased to say that the same steel now is to be found in more peaceful and good households during suitable holidays and used for carving its only victim, the festive bird, rather than as a sword hacking away at an enemy on a bloody battlefield.

As for the Finns I've known, as a people they don't enjoy fighting, but they certainly know how to when it becomes necessary. Much as the Ukrainians have demonstrated, they have an indomitable will, and as they have proved to the world, can be a formidable foe when fighting for the preservation and independence of their homeland. When they were invaded by the overwhelmingly larger Soviet Army in late November, 1939, they fought back desperately and so effectively that by mid-March, 1940, they had brought Russia to the negotiating table. The Finns had to give up ten to fifteen percent of their territory to stop the war, but never were subjugated to Soviet rule. Using *mardi* tactics* they stopped the Red Army.

And what about those other NATO members? Are they beyond the scope of Putin's quasi-Napoleonic dreams of

-----

* In those latitudes the Red Army had to stay on the roads. The Finns, in white uniforms, would ski down the slopes and cut a column in half, then set up machine guns and mortars to fire in opposite directions and shoot the segments to bits with enfilade fire. The Soviets couldn't deploy their armored vehicles off the roads to effective firing positions while the Finns withdrew.

Russian ascendance? With several thousand Russian troops already in the semi-independent region of Transnistria, along Moldova's eastern border, the Baltic States, Poland, Hungary, Romania, Slovakia, Moldova itself, the Czech Republic, Bulgaria, what of them? If I were a Californian I think I'd say that Putin, mad or sane, wants the whole enchilada. He has been in power for twenty years, and based upon his age and his autocratic grip on the leadership of Russia, barring another Russian revolution or some other unforeseen twist of fate, he's got ten more years to pursue his grandiose objectives. I don't think I have to remind anyone that he probably also has a nuclear arsenal larger than ours and the delivery means to send those warheads on their way.* I should remind you also, however, that China, if it has not yet achieved the status of a world superpower, rapidly is becoming one, and with her unwavering intentions about her reacquisition of Taiwan cannot be depended upon to offer any deterrence to Putin's seeming objectives. And now Iran and somewhat ironically, Turkey, that is a member of NATO, seem to be moving toward an *entent cordial* with Russia.†

Let's get back to the home front, but staying with the subject of war. Admittedly, another civil war or a revolution

---

* On April 20th, 2022, Russia announced and showed on film the launching of a hypersonic ballistic missile (ICBM) capable of carrying and directing several nuclear warheads, and its own anti-interdiction device. U.S. officials admitted we have no defense against such a weapon and added, "we're working on it," which in R&D speech means we may have done some research but no development. It also means the weapon, once launched, is unstoppable by any defensive system in our present arsenal of weapons.
† Iran already is shipping munition-armed UAVs (Unmanned Aerial Vehicles) to Russia.

would be disastrous and probably would sound the death knell for our form of democracy, whatever the outcome. Having had some experience as an operations and planning staff officer, I can attest with certitude that organizing, recruiting, equipping, and training a fighting force within the very nation where it would be committed would be a herculean task, if not a fundamentally impossible one.

And then there is the *casus belli*, the justification for war, or in this case the *bellum domesticum*. In that bloody Civil War of 160 years ago, there are to be found a few similarities in its root causes that can be applied to the perilous times we are experiencing today. Other than issues of race, States' rights (or wrongs?) and cupidity, the worshipping of wealth with almost religious fervor, that last evolving into a kind of bastard class system, the overall and more tangible or mundane conditions are quite different. Perhaps instead of States' rights I should have said "influence," when the people's representatives of today, both State and Federal, especially those of virtually every State with a Republican Governor—and there are as many as twenty of them—are adamantly opposed to the passage of a just voters' rights law, outlawing redistricting (gerrymandering), or doing away with filibustering, and joined by the great majority of other Republicans in the Senate. Are we giving life to one of James Madison's greatest fears, that of "…a major or minority of the whole, who are united and actuated by some common impulse of passion, or of interest, averse to the rights of citizens, or to the permanent and aggregate interests of the community"?

5

Let us begin with geography per se, and then, more definitively, domestic political geography. When the CSA (Confederate States of America) began organizing for war they consisted mainly of an enclave in the southeastern part of the country, with eleven seceded southern states and including Texas in the southwest. The southern states later became known as the "Solid South," and in which, from 1879 to 1948 caused Republican opposition to the Democratic Party to be ineffective or negligible. Of as much importance was its political geography, or homogeneity, that factor concerning boundaries of a State and other units for regional or local administration, and for the location of principal administrative centers within the units. The CSA had a President (Jefferson Davis), its own flag (the Stars and Bars), and not of least importance trained officers, graduates of the Military Academy at West Point, with probably the best general in the field on either side, Robert Edward Lee, who knew how to choose his subordinate commanders and senior staff officers. Lee's choices of strategy and tactics also were brilliant, despite his relatively inadequate resources in personnel and logistics. Especially in matters of transportation and communications would the insurgents be stymied, since they have everything to do with planning and operations. As to the rank and file of today's potential insurrectionist "troops," except for those who had served in the Federal armed forces, or to a lesser extent a State National Guard or Reserve unit, it would be almost insane to send them into battle on an OJT basis (on the job training). So however whole-souled their dedication to that Trumpery MAGA (Make America Great Again) may be, an "army" of modern-day insurrectionists would lose every encounter, with heavy losses, to their more adequately trained and equipped adversaries. Those Proud Boys, Oath Keepers, and First Amendment Praetorians may be proficient hunters, but game don't shoot back.

Who or what would comprise the opposed forces? On one side would be the central government as it now stands, to include its armed forces, assuming those forces remain loyal to the Federal cause and to the Constitution they swore to defend and uphold. With some twelve million personnel under arms and with supporting units, a navy with some dozen aircraft carriers and their escort vessels, an air force with state-of-the-art aircraft of all kinds, and several million trained and equipped ground forces and their supporting units, always assuming that these massive forces were completely loyal to the existing government, it would hardly be a fair contest. On the other side would be a geographically disparate foe consisting of doubtful leadership, relatively untrained troops, no offshore forces or organized air support, no known plan for logistical support; in short, a total imbalance in the opposing forces would exist; and this takes us to the loyalties and composition of the rebel forces. Which of our States would participate in such a rebellion, and where would they lie in relation to one another? If a provisional government and its leadership were established, where would it be located? And not of least importance, what of the loyalty of its militias, the State National Guard and the Federal Reserve units?

What about the allegiance of the Federal armed forces? To ascertain that vital information would require, on both sides, a tremendous effort of investigation, counterintelligence, and undercover work in vetting the participants. One can only hope that the FBI and the CIA (as well as the other sixteen intelligence agencies under the Director of National Intelligence) on behalf of our staggering but somehow still standing central government, would be coordinating, talking to one another, as they should have done to prevent the 9/11 catastrophe. Admittedly, such an essential task would be challenging, despite the fact that most of the senior officers in the armed forces would be loyal to the oaths they had taken when they were commissioned. Those who were not probably would retire, and their subsequent activities given some attention. That is not to say that should the pro-Trump Republicans take control of Congress and the Executive Branch of government by 2024, giving them power to replace Cabinet appointees, there would not be the possibility of collusion between the potential insurgents and the Department of Defense, which includes all the armed forces.*

In those uncertain years of the early 1960s, with that controversial Zapruder film of Kennedy's assassination being made public, another film was released in 1964, this one made in Hollywood. The movie was titled *Seven*

---

* This includes even the U.S. Coast Guard, which in peacetime comes under the jurisdiction of the Department of Transportation but reverts to the Department of Defense in wartime.

Days in May, featuring such "stars" as Burt Lancaster, Kirk Douglas, and Frederick March (as the U.S. President). The plot centered on an attempted *coup d'etat* led by no one less than the Chairman of the Joint Chiefs of Staff (Lancaster) and his high-ranking cronies here and abroad, Ultimately, the plot was foiled, in almost predictable Hollywood style, by the revelation of the meticulously planned *coup* in a cigarette case found at the scene of an airline crash site where there were no survivors, that and the able assistance of the true-blue loyal Marine Colonel (Douglas), who was the Chief's executive assistant, and who in turn was aided by his Chief's former mistress (La Gardner). Having watched the movie I decided that it was more *coup d' theatre* than anything else. Still, whatever else one would wish to call it, and it was fiction and at that time improbable; that is not to say that today such a scenario would be impossible. The first step in the rebels' plan, which was to take control of all radio and TV stations (there was no internet in 1964), made the film more credible to me.

It should be apparent if not obvious that because of the overwhelming imbalances between the opposing forces a civil war victory for the rebels would be a forlorn hope. Might they have any success in attempting to foment a revolution by the general population as we did in freeing ourselves from the bonds of England, or as the French did in 1789 to free themselves from a tyrannical monarchy? Here we must deal in demographics, in numbers. We have been told repeatedly by the news outlets that the claque of Trump supporters in this country numbers about seventy-five or eighty million voters. Were I planning a national rebellion,

I would welcome such a statistic. But in the case of a civil war there would be difficulties even in its conception. In France in 1789, as in Lang's *Metropolis*, the rich played while millions were literally starving, with bread lines everywhere in the cities, no matter what Marie Antoinette may have said, however innocently, about giving them cake if they had no bread. And in our own revolution a dozen or so years earlier than that in France, a war between thirteen British North American colonies and their mother country, resulting from British acts of imposing taxes and regulations (what the rebellious are calling "mandates" here today) which they regarded as tyrannical and produced a growing sense of nationalism and righteous power among the colonists, there grew a decisive willingness to rebel against England. Remember what I have said about attitudes; they remain only that unless they lead to behavior, action. Remember also what Pascal said centuries ago: "Justice without power is helpless; power without justice is tyranny." To sum up, I trust it is possible, perhaps even probable, depending on a just outcome of the 1/6 committee's investigations and hearings on the abominable attack on the Capitol, that while there may be more such incidents of a greater or lesser degree, neither a civil nor a revolutionary war lies in our foreseeable future. Meanwhile, so many Americans are asking about this seemingly endless pandemic, as do so many children on a journey in the back seat of a car ask of their apathetic parents: "Are we there yet?" In the chaotic condition we find ourselves today that would be a trenchant question. There? Where *is* "there"? Where should we want to go? And of even more importance, where *could* we go?

It is becoming difficult to distinguish the good news from the bad news. Well, I can tell you about some news we have been hearing concerning the war in Ukraine that seems intended to be in favor of the Ukrainians in their courageous and desperate battle against the Russian invaders. Not infrequently, interviews are broadcast between American reporters and Ukrainian officials who have informative, accurate, and useful answers to the questions they have put to them. If the answers seem optimistic and favorable for the Ukrainians the audience can be expected to consider this as good news. It may have been informative and accurate, but to whom? I think it would be safe to say that neither the interviewing journalist nor, with very few exceptions, the person being interviewed has little, if any, knowledge of the process of intelligence production. Unless an intelligence operative is handling a reliable source or agent, raw information is gathered by analysts and evaluators. After that information has been analyzed and evaluated according to its source and reliability it may become useful intelligence. At times however, the source might be of unwitting use to the enemy. On a CNN TV interview recently the interviewer asked Ukraine's Minister for Infrastructure if President Biden's promised and substantial aid in weapons and ammunition was having any trouble getting into Ukraine, and specified what NATO countries they were coming from. Now if the Russian intelligence community isn't monitoring every bit of news about the war, especially that coming out of the U.S., they understand as little about intelligence production as that interviewer, and for the matter of that, the poor fellow who was being interviewed. How many roads or rail systems are there between Ukraine's border and Country X or Y? Are those routes still useable? We have satellite photography; can we interdict them? Where? What might be the destination of that "lethal aid"? And as long as I'm sounding this horn of warning, there is this. All the TV news outlets have been putting up graphics showing an itemized list of the items the Ukrainians can expect to receive, and they have been doing it with hardly any lapse of time after the White House made its detailed announcement. Always tell your enemy what to expect, right? Wrong: let him find out when it's blowing him to bits. It seems incredible that at least one of our seventeen intelligence agencies hasn't been ringing White House (and CNN's) phones off the hook. As to operations, I have this to say. If the Russians continue to fire ordnance from within their own borders and those of their ally Belarus, why have we not provided the Ukrainians with the counterbattery radar we have available to pinpoint the locations of the missile launching and artillery positions so they can pay the Russians back in their own coin? What do borders matter when two adjacent countries are at war? Did Russia show any deference to Ukraine's borders when she invaded her, or when she made that incursion into the Donbas region eight years ago?

As for that no-fly zone that President Zelensky keeps begging for, is not the air above Ukraine, a sovereign nation, entitled to the same rights as its marginal seas?* If we remain

---

* Aerial domain is space beginning at the terrestrial surface and continuing outward through the stratosphere into the ionosphere and beyond. For an undetermined distance immediately beyond the terrestrial surface, space is held to fall within the jurisdiction of the nation controlling the surface.

adamantly opposed to providing air support but one or more of our NATO allies would be willing to do it, I say let them do it. If the aircraft were provided, the Ukrainians would fly them, and would it not be poetically just if those planes were those MIG-29s left in those former Iron Curtain nations that now are members of the European Union and NATO? In any case, even a hardened veteran at this point in this vicious, unbalanced, and totally unjustified war would say, Enough! there's been enough slaughter of innocent people, and I include most of those young Russian soldiers who are dying as pawns in Putin's mad pursuit of power.

In this persistent, ever-changing, seemingly endless pandemic 2500 people were dying every day, while medical scientists hoped fervently that existing vaccines would be able to control a variant that they named Omicron. The daily death toll has dropped to 1000 a day, but overall deaths kept moving steadily beyond the million mark, and we are being warned that the daily rate may rise again. Only about twenty-four to thirty-eight percent of the population have received all the vaccinations and booster shots. The remainder have not for a number of reasons, but mainly because being mandated to submit would be an abridgement of their democratic rights to their personal liberty. While most people think that life, anyone's life, is too precious to lose unnecessarily, I am more pragmatic about the matter. I say unequivocally that with the exception of those who have a valid medical or religious reason for not doing so, all should be made to be vaccinated, less for their own sakes than for the innocent people they may be infecting. The only small satisfaction I get from the current state of affairs is that the deaths of those intractable cretins who refuse vaccination for no valid reason will be no great loss to our society. Now there are reports that yet a second booster and perhaps even a third shot may be needed to mitigate the current B-5 surge that a number of other countries are beginning to experience, and we're being told by reliable sources that there will be more variants coming. Now let us take a few more brief divergences in our ramble.

6

Before they were preempted by the Russo-Ukrainian conflict I watched, *ad nauseum*, those film clips of the chaotic attack on the Capitol. I watched also those interviews reporters conducted with those forsworn Trump devotees, both male and female. With few exceptions, those Trump-beguiled nincompoops have similar characteristics, both physical and mental; they generally are obese, and from their replies about their beliefs give me the impression that their IQs match their ages. You may recall here what I've said about the state of literacy in this country, or perhaps I should say illiteracy. In the case of these people it is a major problem in clear or right thinking. The "progressive" namby-pamby Democrats who insist that we are all equal, both physically and mentally, only exacerbate the problem. And as Alexander Pope said, "A little learning is a dangerous thing." The only good news about all this is that in the event of any attempted *coup d'état*, these upstarts would have difficulty finding good leaders, leaders such as the rebels had in Robert E. Lee during our bloody Civil War. I'm sorry to end this by saying that all levels of law enforcement, except for the actors who play them on all those police procedurals, our policemen and women are as fat as those Proud Boys, et al; they have to shoot suspects in situations when they should chase and subdue them. There will be more about this as we go on.

America has become known as, among several other unflattering titles, the United States of Addiction as that sub-epidemic of opiate use and its resultant deaths continue increasingly to sweep the country.* Of the drugs available to users, none have a deadlier effect nor are more available to users than Methamphetamine and Fentanyl. "It's everywhere, all over the streets," said one self-proclaimed addict when interviewed in Fresno, California. The devil is a busy man; but remember also that basic rule of economics about supply and *demand.*

Then there was this sudden rash of "smash and grab" robberies across the country. Admittedly, I'm a born skeptic; I believe in conspiracies, and there have been hundreds if not thousands in recorded history. Could these events, seemingly organized and coordinated, have been motivated by something other than, or in addition to simple looting for criminal gain? Could they have been connected somehow to the political controversy of whether to raise or reduce funding for police throughout the nation? Whatever the case, having seen film clips of some of the events themselves, I could suggest that some attention be given, aside from the mob of felons dressed in black, to the one wearing a white "hoody," and in another robbery a red one, much as a leader in combat wears some insignia for identification on the back of his helmet. Other than that I suggest that police responders be permitted to shoot the looters on sight.

Also in keeping with our self-inspired problems is what is seen by almost the whole world as our insane tolerance of privately owned firearms. Not long ago, four were killed and seven wounded (or as the news outlets prefer to call

---

* Or, with our thousands killed in senseless shootings, the United States of Assassination.

it, "injured") at a Michigan school by a fifteen-year-old boy whose parents gave him a pistol for his birthday. This makes a total of more than 360 mass shootings thus far this year (August 2022). There have been more than 150,000 deaths by gunshot in this country in the last four years. As always, the FBI and local police in their investigations are concentrating on the "causes of the incident" while the root cause, that of gun control, or more precisely its lack, is avoided or just ignored.* In certain relatively lesser cases, the

---

* As I've said elsewhere a number of times, if we can't control the firearms, we can, and should, restrict the sale or availability of the ammunition most commonly used in these wanton shootings. Two examples are 5.56mm (.223 caliber) for Colt's AR-15 and all 9 and 10mm pistol ammunition, with proper allowances for the armed forces and law enforcement personnel. As a camera is useless without film, so is a gun without ammunition. In enacting and enforcing the laws necessary to establish restrictions on the availability of ammunition to private firearms owners, certain collateral aspects of such a mandate must be taken into consideration. The first of these would be provision for the requirements of our armed forces and law enforcement agencies. Such supply must be carefully monitored, controlled and recorded. Another lies in the practice of self-loading or reloading ammunition. There are four components to small arms cartridges: a brass case, a bullet, the explosive charge that drives the bullet, and a primer centered at the base of the cartridge case or casings. Without exception you'll hear on TV and in movies that the brass cases that are found at a crime scene are referred to as "shell cases"; that may be so if they were referring to shotgun shells or those of an artillery piece, but not the expended brass of small arms firing. Nonetheless, those empty cartridge cases can be reused. Care must be taken in selecting those that are not dented or scarred in any way, to avoid stoppages when reused, and the expended primers can be replaced by machines designed for that purpose, as well as those that replace the projectiles and the proper main charge. The reason that reloading could be a problem in the restriction of ammunition is that it could give rise to an underground industry of reloading. Rim-fired .22 caliber "shorts" such as those used in erstwhile shooting galleries should also be banned.

same FBI has demonstrated its ineffectuality: in the matter of the molestation and child abuse of those female gymnasts by the late Dr. Nassar, et al, by stalling and ignoring the investigation for at least a year; by ignoring the evidence that would have enabled them to avoid the gunslinging tragedy in that Parkland school shooting in Florida; and in the search for Gabby Petito by not questioning the parents of Brian Laundrie as a first step in their investigation. There will be more on enforcement and judiciary matters anon.

While the reportage from Ukraine continues to dominate the news, we've been spared those stimulating accounts of Captain Kirk and his journey into "space," Britney Spears' court trials, and missing or inconvenienced tennis stars. We did have news of the late whoreson Jeffrey Epstein and his child procurer, Ghislane Maxwell. Relatively little publicity was given to Prince Andrew, second son of Queen Elizabeth II, one-time friend of Epstein's and alleged participant in the pedophilia scandals surrounding Epstein and La Maxwell. Mention of that Royal House of Windsor prompts a little interesting history. Originally the House of Sax-Coberg Goethe (the Kings George), the name was replaced by "Windsor" in 1915 when England was at war with Germany and Windsor was chosen as being more suitable and patriotic. This was at a time when little dachschunds and miniature schnauzers were being kicked to death in London's streets and while in the U.S. sauerkraut was renamed "liberty cabbage." Although Queen Victoria spoke German when with her mother and later to her German husband, Prince Consort Albert, she thought it more suitable to speak English to almost everyone else. I continue to wonder why, when we were deluged with filmed coverage of the late Princess Diana's other grandchildren almost immediately after their births, Prince Harry's and Princess Meghan's latest child wasn't revealed for weeks, perhaps months, after her arrival. When the baby finally was shown there was nothing remarkable about her, probably to the chagrin of the white supremacists here in America, who were hoping that that House of "Windsor" wished to preserve that *tabula rasa* (clean slate) of 1000 years of white progeny.

As I explained in my brief apologia about this dissertation, you should now understand what I meant by presenting a continuum of facts and events without the rigorous, cohesiveness I would have liked to provide. In other words, history is moving so quickly today that an interested observer finds it difficult if not impossible to stay with one subject until it is fully or adequately explained, since pertinent events change in a matter of hours if not minutes, and these events in good part have become momentous. If this were journalistic reporting, you would be seeing lead-in phrases such as "This just in" or "Breaking news," and I even may resort to that if I feel I must at certain times. You will find some segment history-cum-current events in certain passages, but no rigorous cohesiveness, and few "patchwork quilts."

One can only hope that those 1/6 hearings and investigations don't follow the traditional and time-consuming examples we have had to endure in proceedings of all such inquiries by our organs of government in all its branches. One thinks of the labors of Sisyphus in trying to get that massive rock up and over the top of that hill with the same fruitless result. In a more common American vernacular, our proceedings, especially those of our judiciary system are similar to trying to move molasses uphill on a very cold day. If the special committee does not reach a satisfactory conclusion on the side of justice before those midterm elections in the fall of 2022, the results could be dire for the Democrats, and that is to say nothing of the 2024 presidential election. It is already conceivable that the Republicans will regain both Houses of Congress in 2022 and that Trump, if he isn't indicted for incitement to riot and sedition, or worse, will run for and even win back the Presidency two years later. Time, or precisely its waste, has become one of our silent but deadliest enemies and we ourselves will have encouraged that enemy. The dictum "slow and steady wins the race" has no application in this case anymore than it applies to winning the war against the virus, with all its variants.

7

In our maximum effort during World War II, work increased its pace commensurately. Work in factories increased threefold with round the clock day, swing, and night shifts. With so many men off to fight the war and these increased efforts to raise productivity there was no unemployment problem (witness "Rosie the Riveter"). Risking the disapproval of certain of his devotees, it is a fact that despite his good intentions and his programs to alleviate its miseries it was our entering the war, not FDR, (excepting his collusion with Churchill), that finally pulled us out of the Great Depression.

Why must Federal employees, especially those in the top levels of all three branches, take so much time off? Members of Congress will tell you they must go back to their home States in order to be available to confer with their constituents. Actually they go back to do some campaigning for the next election. Let their constituents communicate with them, especially in these times when the internet makes communicating so easy. Why must the Supreme Court take that months-long break every year? In the heat of a war, members of the armed forces get leave only for emergencies, such as being incapacitated by wounds. We are now fighting in a grave emergency, but we continue to act as if these were "normal" times. How can the Government justify this dilatory inattention to duty for the general public they should be serving? Our problems will persist until we find viable solutions to them; then we must fight the all-in battles to achieve them. If we go on merely talking about our problems, we will end by committing a form of collective national suicide. And if climate change ultimately sends us all to perdition at least we'll have the small satisfaction that we went down swinging.

If you are as wearied as I in airing our domestic problems perhaps we should take a ramble abroad for a time. I suggest that we travel by ship. "Getting there can be part of the fun," the travel agents could say before the advent of the commercial jet. Today, unless you're in a hurry to get somewhere (time is money) and can afford to fly first class, shipboard travel still leaves flying at the gate, if you'll allow the little play on words. Any seasoned traveler, not tourist, for there is no comparing the two, who is reasonably fit physically and for whom time is no constraint, would agree with me, unless he were prone to *mal de mer*. A traveler wouldn't want to be seen, however, in or on one of those currently popular cruise ships, that he would view as a great but grotesque floating hotel stuffed to its bilges with uninteresting yahoos and calling briefly at a few ports but having no specific destination. A true traveler will have a specific destination (but must be flexible enough to adjust this should he or she be abroad a tramp steamer, which may be diverted enroute to pick up cargo elsewhere, if tramp steamers still exist). Since I have not been at sea (except metaphorically) for many years, I don't know whether maritime law still requires that there be accommodations for twelve passengers aboard every freighter or cargo ship under any nation's flag (it might be a "monkey flag" such as Singapore's or some other country with low registration rates). I do know that in 1991 I sailed from Newport News, Virginia to Brazil in a German bulk carrier. As the sole passenger, I was fortunate enough to occupy the spacious and deluxe cabin reserved for none other than the President of the shipping line in the event that he should want to observe the ship's operations first-hand. With a slight grin, the ship's Captain told me he never had.

If time is your friend and not your foe, travel by sea does have certain advantages over flying in a sealed capsule, breathing processed air, and confined, more or less, to a seat in close proximity to several hundred other people, all of whom, if you are traveling alone, strangers. On a ship we would have time to prepare ourselves for what we are to find before we disembark at some port of entry such as Southamton, La Harve, Hong Kong, or Yokohama. Those of us who have more than one language can brush it or them up with the stewards or foreign passengers. As we watch the playful dolphins and flying fish leading the ship on her way we also can fill our lungs with that fresh, salty, sea air. Passengers aboard ship can walk the decks freely if they are so inclined, or even jog if they are able to; while a number of us would enjoy settling in a deck chair with a good book. Yes, this would be a good opportunity to become reacquainted with that foreign language you studied in high school or college, as well as to learn a little about the history and culture of the place(s) you intend to visit. I hope this digression may be useful or at least of some interest to you.

8

One of our greatest impediments in structuring, implementing, and conducting our foreign relations has been our inability to converse with people of other nations in their native tongues, especially when we are in their own countries. But perhaps "inability" was somewhat misleading; a general reluctance would have been a better way to phrase what I want to say. That reluctance is rooted in indifference and in arrogance, an arrogance that is tinged with xenophobia, and that has been very costly to us in all our foreign relations. Witness our disgraceful withdrawal from Afghanistan, with seventy-eight-thousand Afghans, mainly translators and interpreters, left to their grim fate under the newly reinstated Taliban regime.*

Too many people are too ready to ascribe our linguistic disabilities to our geographic remoteness from the rest of the world due to being flanked by two great oceans. That may have served to some extent in the past, but with the progress that has been made in transportation and communications this has become utter nonsense. The actual reasons for our linguistic liabilities are to be found in our third-rate public

---

* The Army had a Foreign Language school in California (Monterey or Ft. Mason?) during the cold war. If it's still there, we're being very quiet about it. Many years ago one of the news weeklies carried a feature article on this subject which included a sidebar "quiz" "What do we call someone who speaks two languages? Bilingual. Three languages? Trilingual. Only one? American." There was a time, during the nineteenth and halfway through the twentieth centuries when medical students had to learn German and Latin, and attorneys had to be conversant with Latin.

educational system (remember those illiteracy statistics),* laziness, arrogant exceptionalism, and yes, a pervasive, downright xenophobia among too many in our "democratic" populace. With this and several other amateurish disabilities in mind, how can we declare ourselves to be the leader of the free world? The answer to that trenchant question lies out West, within the silos that contain those devil's devices of mutually assured destruction.

Even when one travels abroad certain matters of interest seem to cling to him. One of these, to the traveler who has an interest in the law and politics, might be the Supreme Court's hearing on the abortion laws in Mississippi, along with those enacted in Texas in the recent past. Eventually, such a hearing has led to the high court's decision to rescind that fifty-year-old Roe V Wade law and will give each state the right to enact its own abortion laws; that would require women in some states, even in cases of rape or incest, to travel as far as hundreds of miles to have the procedure performed. This is another example of the need for a Constitutional change, since its Fourteenth Amendment, used as a basis for the Roe V Wade decision, was in its original and essential intent, used as a basis for providing rights to former slaves freed by the Emancipation Proclamation. It can be argued (and was) that the wording of the Amendment is too tenuous and vague to be applied to women's personal rights and liberty. We will hear more about the Court's decision(s) later, but based upon its composition, even now that Biden's liberal appointee Ketanji Brown Jackson has replaced retired

---

* As James Madison said, "a well-instructed people alone can be a permanently free people."

Associate Justice Stephen Breyer the future of women's rights to abortions appears dim. Nowhere in the Constitution is there a "right to privacy," nor, to my knowledge, does even the word "privacy" appear.

There are times when a little history can be helpful, even necessary, to understand and assess current events. After that bracing sea voyage and arrival in Europe, our ramble took us to the Belarus-Polish border where hordes of refugees were trying, mainly unsuccessfully, to cross into Poland to escape the pro-Russian oppression in their homeland. Concomitantly, Russia was massing troops along her border with Belarus. To the south, Russia had positioned some 120,000 troops (the number seemed to vary daily) along their entire border with Ukraine. They already had been making "intrusions" into eastern Ukraine for eight years, and it was reported that there already were some 34,000 Russian soldiers wearing Ukrainian uniforms among the Russian sympathizers in the Donbas region of eastern Ukraine. Having repossessed the Crimea, Russia now wanted a corridor, or "land bridge" from Ukraine to the Crimean Peninsula. Reports abounded that the Russians might conduct "false flag" operations: Russians in Ukrainian uniforms "attacking" their own forces as justification for an actual invasion.

If actual hostilities broke out between the United States and Russia, the other NATO nations would be required by their Charter to join in the fray. But would they be willing to do that with two opposing arsenals of nuclear weapons waiting in the wings? And keep this in mind: without those military satellites circling the globe, no nation could wage a successful war.* There would be no victor in a nuclear war except the war itself. And then there is our domestic state of affairs. Are we, with all our disunity and crises at home, especially with that crippling divide in public opinion, in any condition to fight a major war, even if it were a "conventional" non-nuclear one?

Following our shameful departure from Afghanistan, President Biden, as Commander-in-Chief, made two seminal errors, both in regard to the war in Ukraine. The first lay in that second title that the Constitution bestows on all Presidents. When he was in Poland and the Russians were destroying cities and towns all over Ukraine, he was asked by President Zelensky to visit him in Kyiv. He turned down the invitation with his regrets. When asked by the press why he refused to go he replied somewhat deferentially and with a slight smile: "'They' won't let me go." They? Once can only assume that he was alluding to the head of his security detail and to others of his closest advisors. This is analogous to a Regimental Commander being told by his Chief of Staff and other staff officers that he can't visit his troops in the front lines. I can hear that Regimental CO telling those well-meaning subordinates something akin to: "Look here, I appreciate your concern for my safety, but I don't think it would lower their morale if those boys up there saw the old

---

* The Russians claim they have developed a system to destroy those satellites. Perhaps they have, but what concerns me more is that we have proof positive that they now have available a hypersonic ballistic missile capable of reaching speeds in the Mach-5 to even Mach-10 range (five to ten times the speed of sound). The North Koreans surpassed the Russians earlier with their own missile. We have no such weapon nor the means to defend against. it.

man among them for awhile. Send for my driver." End of discussion. If Biden isn't the boss as Commander-in-Chief who in hell is? Meanwhile, Zelensky received a number of high-ranking visitors, to include a Foreign Prime Minister or two, and after a relatively long length of time, the U.S. deigned to send its Secretaries of State and Defense, after an impenetrable cloak of secrecy as to their expected time of arrival, to talk with the truly heroic, beleaguered President Zelensky who once again literally beseeched them to send him more military aid as quickly as possible.

The second error, which has proved to be immensely more important, at least in a material sense, was not so totally the fault of the President. Our cumbersome system of government, with all its institutional delays in getting virtually anything done, deserves a good deal of the blame. While thousands of innocent Ukrainians were being slaughtered or displaced, Congress, in its typically ponderous way, finally passed the necessary legislation to fund aid for the now desperate Ukrainians, while the Department of Defense could have been packing and loading C-17 cargo planes for anticipated flights to Poland, from which the needed armaments could be transshipped to Ukraine. When approval finally came, we did the Russians the great favor, over network and cable news outlets, of telling the world just what we were sending, giving the invaders enough time to identify the points of probable entry and the roads and railways that would be used to get the supplies to the Ukrainian forces, an intelligence blunder that should go down in the history of wars. As important as revealing where the supply chain could be interdicted, the Russians had been told in detail what weapons the Ukrainians would receive and so could plan to counter and defend against them; more than enough to make an enemy's intelligence officers cheer while ours wept with frustration and dismay. In any case what we have given the Ukrainians is too little, too late. Fear of escalation resulting in a nuclear war, the U.S. and its NATO allies have erred on the side of caution, even timidity, and not least, perhaps even mainly, on our misplaced sense of Justice.

Our unremitting support of Israel, despite her continued atrocities against the Palestinians they dispossessed three-quarters of a century ago is in great part the cause of the "Islamic terrorism" we have brought upon ourselves. In 1973, five years after they purposely had attacked the U.S. surveillance ship *Liberty* with aircraft and torpedo boats off their coast (beyond the twelve-mile limit) during the Six-Day War, which left thirty-four Americans dead and 171 wounded, and during their Yom Kippur War, we virtually emptied the shelves of our conventional weapons and sent them to "our greatest ally in the Middle East" (which permits us to have only the *pro forma* small detachment of U.S. Marines at our embassy in Jerusalem as our only armed force in their entire country). That can be added to other outrageous acts we have committed in the Middle East. To list a few of these: the CIA-conducted *coup d'état* in 1953 that reinstated the deposed, despotic Shah of Iran; the disintegration of Iraq after our ill-founded invasion and occupation of that nation; the fruitless occupation of Afghanistan for twenty years; our virtual abandonment of the Syrians to the Assad regime; abrogation of a nuclear arms treaty with Iran (at the irrepressible insistance of Israel, their arch enemy); fist bumps rather than fisticuffs between Biden and Mohammed Bin Salman (MBS) of Saudi Arabia, whence came fifteen of the nineteen men who attacked the World Trade Towers, and more recently the MBS-inspired killing and dismembering of a U.S. citizen; our indifference to the continued effort of the same Saudi Arabia that is striving to kill or starve to death those rebels in Yemen, on and on. I could have mentioned the infamous Iran-Contra Affair during the Reagan era, but this isn't a history book *per se*.

Our complete disregard of Justice in this area, driven by motives of power and avarice, and blatant xenophobia, can in some ways be compared to the havoc caused by the Christian Crusades of the 11th, 12th, and 13th centuries to win The Holy Land from the Muslims. Can you not see that the turmoil in the Middle East is largely of our own making? And we can assassinate as many of those Muslim leaders, good or bad, that we can boast about; there will always be another waiting in the wings to replace him, if not immediately, then not much later. We won't be able to quell the "terrorists" unless or until we adopt a just foreign policy in the region.

Another lengthy digression, yes, but one that I trust will help to reveal some of the less appreciated spaces in the larger canvas of our international relations. And recall what George Kennan said after World War II and at the beginning of the Cold War: "We must always have an enemy; if we don't have one, we invent one."

9

When the news outlets become excessively repetitious and increase their coverage of other events that are relatively minor you can be certain that the war in Ukraine is not progressing in Ukraine's favor. Lately, we've been hearing too much about the former U.S. Marine who was killed while fighting for the Ukrainians and of the former Marine who was released from a Russian prison in a prisoner exchange. As usual, while thousands of innocent people are being killed and wounded that is merely to be regretted, but when an American is in any kind of jeopardy, well, that's "different."

Similarly, if in a different context, while Ukrainian mothers were trying to shelter with their infant children from Russian artillery and rocket fire in the rubble of that steel mill in Mariupol and had been for weeks without the necessities of human survival, CNN announced that American mothers could not find the formula milk their infants prefer due to shortages in the supply chain. American mothers complained that this made their infants cross and unruly. What should we say to those Ukrainian mothers whose breast milk had dried up and who were grateful to find a few ounces of clean water to prevent their babies from dying of dehydration? The absence of the other necessities needed to go on with sustainable life is almost unimaginable. This conscienceless disregard for the misfortunes of "others," and callous self-centered indifference would be difficult to find anywhere but here, in my native country. That was difficult enough to say, but I must add that the even darker and more shameful aspect of this is that the average American mother who is complaining about the lack of Similac wouldn't or couldn't last a day of what their valiant Ukrainian counterparts have endured for weeks or even months.*

From the Baltic Sea to the Adriatic, Joseph Stalin's Iron Curtain descended over eastern Europe following the Second World War. The North Atlantic Treaty Organization, commonly known as NATO, was formed on August 24th, 1949, to preclude further encroachment and to defend against it should it occur, with twelve original members. Over the years, after the Balkan Wars and then the collapse of the Soviet Union, and the reunification of Germany, eighteen more members were admitted to the Organization; none of its present thirty nation-states have left. Ukraine, with a population of about 45 million people and with what probably was the best army in Europe, wanted to join NATO but was refused membership. If it had been accepted, either the Russians would not have invaded her, or if they had we would be at war with the Russians, as would the rest of the NATO nations (NATO Article Five-war with one, war with all). The reason NATO

---

* In February 2022, Abbott, which supplies most of the formula in the U.S., revealed that its product was contaminated. Word of this didn't reach President Biden until early April, as he has alleged. By the 27th of May, seventy percent of all formula was out of stock. Now we have had to rely on other countries such as Great Britain, Germany, and far away Australia to help us in yet another crisis. We should nationalize the pharmaceutical industry, to include formula milk, to say nothing of life-sustaining drugs for the general populace that cost eight times more than they do in any other civilized nation.

refused her membership almost certainly was that Ukraine was considered to be a "buffer state," among others in that southeast corner of Europe. Simply put, NATO was on the horns of a dilemma, and made the wrong choice, mainly because they did not have any knowledge of President Putin's mind-set and his grandiose schemes for the destiny of Russia. His megalomania has now led us to the brink of a nuclear war.

But let us pause here for a few moments to clarify some terms. A dilemma is a situation involving choice between equally unsatisfactory alternatives: in this case either to admit Ukraine into NATO or let it serve as a buffer state between Russia and the European Union. I think we can assume that NATO, with the fall of the Soviet Union, did not consider they were faced with so potentially great a threat as their confrontation with the USSR had been. A buffer state is a relatively smaller nation that separates great powers whose boundaries would otherwise be contiguous, and which thereby reduces the possibility of friction between the greater powers and provides a potential military barrier. Poland, a member of NATO since March of 1999, was a buffer state between Germany and Russia for years until by treaty it was divided in two, with each of those two powers taking half. That was a case of a smaller state occupying a territory which neighboring great powers may covet for strategic or other reasons, but which neither dares to annex because of mutual rivalry or distrust. Had they have had more foresight and awareness of Putin's intentions, NATO, to include the U.S., should have begun arming Ukraine with the weapons and other war aid they are giving them now, when the Russians annexed the Crimea and then began occupying the Donbas Region eight years ago. Better still, they should have allowed Ukraine to join NATO before those portentous events ever occurred. In any case, now we've got to share the butcher's bill, to some extent anyway, with President Putin.

I could suggest that what we can do now is to impose the only effective sanction on Russia, one that should have been used at the beginning of hostilities in Ukraine, and that is to cut off all fossil fuel products, most especially natural gas, that Russia supplies to Europe, a sanction which would exceed all those in place now put together. Let the Germans go back to those lovely tile stoves and others to their own devices. After all, summer is on the way.*

If we must forgo the pleasures and benefits of travel by sea, and wish to avoid the inconveniences of crossing international borders, using trains or other land transport, we might take an airline flight to Afghanistan, although we might have to disguise ourselves to look like anyone but an American after our infamous departure from that country.

Our primary objective when we went in there, unbidden and uninvited, in 2001 as we have done in other nations throughout the world from time to time, twenty years ago, it was to rid the country of Al Qaeda, which was using the place as a training and operational base (in Arabic Al Qaeda literally means "the base"). Our motivation for doing

---

* Unfortunately, those infamous Kremlin agents known as the "Wagner Group" are extracting billions of dollars of Sudanese gold, sharing the proceeds with the corrupt and unpopular military government there, and sending the bulk to Russia to help pursue the war in Ukraine; meanwhile protesters are being killed in the streets of Khartoum.

this was to avenge ourselves for that disastrous 9/11 attack in New York, although the officially stated reason was to prevent any future similar events. Of interest is the fact, that is now a general consensus, that the catastrophe in New York as well as that intended for the Capitol but averted by the airline crash in Pennsylvania, could all have been avoided if the CIA and the FBI had cooperated and coordinated their intelligence operations. While we touted our success in the mission, Al-Qaeda obligingly and quietly moved to their new base in Pakistan, our alleged friend, and found sanctuary there. Reveling in our "success" we redirected the mission to one of counterinsurgency and "nation building." In that endeavor we failed completely, as had the British in their two Afghan Wars during the nineteenth century and the Soviet Union during their ten year occupation in more recent history. Alexander the Great could be said to have had more success, but of course he was just passing through on his way to India. Now we have been reduced to the rather feeble justification for twenty years of costly and fruitless endeavor there that at least during that time we have been spared the fear of more attacks on our homeland, which is utter nonsense since such attacks could be planned and carried out from any number of places in the world.

After our humiliating departure, which some U.S. officials preferred to call a NEO (Noncombative Extraction Operation), another euphemistic dodge to avoid what any sensible soldier would call it in much more colorful barrack room language, we have had to admit that we left, in addition to several hundreds of Americans, tens of thousands of Afghan translators, interpreters, and other indigenous people and their families who assisted us in our futile endeavors against the same Taliban regime, now reinstated, that we found there in 2001. Why?; mainly because of the paucity of Americans who can speak, read, or write in any language except English, and in too many cases even that poorly. One would think that every American connected directly or indirectly with the U.S. Government in that ill-fated country had his or her own translator-interpreter. Yes, they may not have loved us, but they'll never forget us. Of course, we did permit their poppy growers to go on with their lucrative trade.

Upon landing at Kabul International Airport, our traveler can see ranked in dozens, U.S. combat and utility vehicles as well as perfectly serviceable helicopters, as are those ground vehicles, all abandoned when the Americans fled the scene in haste and virtual panic. All over the country he would see similar treasure troves, in much greater numbers, worth hundreds of billions of dollars, left to the victorious Taliban. We probably left more munitions, equipment, supplies, and installations in Afghanistan than we did in Vietnam, and what we left there is incalculable: ground transport and fighting vehicles, artillery pieces and myriad other crew served weapons, thousands of individual small arms, tons of ammunition, rations, uniforms, hundreds of aircraft, both rotary and fixed wing, bases, barracks, airfields, hospitals and aid stations with a plethora of medical supplies and equipment, on and on. In Afghanistan, all the Taliban has to do is to train their soldiers and airmen in the use of the more sophisticated equipment. In short, we will have equipped an enemy for battle and for the suppression of the people over whom they once again rule. And now there is a further conflict in this already beleaguered country, between the newly victorious Taliban and what is known as ISIS-K, another orthodox extremist Islamic Caliphate we heard of during the turmoil in Syria, a nation about whose current affairs we have heard nothing of great interest since we left there except for that raid in northeast Syria in which we killed ISIS leader Haji Abdulla. The late syndicated columnist Mark Shields, in an entirely different context, once described such a conflict as a "civil war in a leper colony." In any case, we left the Afghans helpless when they needed sensible assistance desperately. Incidentally, along with Haji Abdulla, the women and children in his house also were killed in that raid.* Of course, we blamed the latter's' deaths on the detonation of a suicide bomb Abdulla was wearing. What we don't seem to realize is that when we assassinate one of these Islamic "terrorist leaders" his successor would take charge almost before the last shot was fired. In any case, the recent earthquake in Afghanistan has dealt the Taliban a blow we couldn't during our twenty-year occupation there; perhaps in this case Mother Nature was working on our behalf.

---

* I may be confusing this event with the killing of Osama Bin Laden, that occurred during the Obama Administration. In any case, it little matters in our continued obfuscation of such misdeeds (recall the My Lai atrocities in the Vietnam War).

$$10$$

No great distance to the northeast of Kabul, beyond the Hindu Kush in the Karakorum Mountain Range, lies modern China, still as much an enigma to the Western mind as to its proclivities and actions as it has been for centuries past. Would it be wise to take another flight there, then to Seoul, Korea, on to Tokyo, and then take ship again for a brief visit to the Antipodes, to our ally Australia, and perhaps even on to Antarctica to witness firsthand the appalling ravages wrought by global warming?

Should we go on with our globe-trotting at all or should we settle our inquiry without being "on the ground," as has become a favorite and nonsensical cliché among newscasters—where in hell else would we be, flying like Superman over the area of interest? Could we merely probe for reasonable answers to some trenchant questions as have journalists for centuries: who, what, when, where, for the front page and never forgetting that "why," which usually is to be found on the op-ed pages if it explains something truthfully, that is at the root of any really important event or matter and should belong on the front page but seldom is? The why of that shooting that killed four people at that Michigan high school should have been answered by: Unlike virtually all civilized nations on the planet we are the only one that has lost all control over privately owned firearms. However unbalanced that teenaged shooter may have been, the killing couldn't have happened without that pistol he possessed. Having borne this brief digression, permit me to go on; and since we've already arrived in China, let us tarry here for a bit. We'll decide later whether to go on from here or to just return home.

China is on the verge of becoming another superpower, and I have this to ask: how would the United States react if Chinese warships began cruising around off both our coasts, in the Caribbean Sea, and even in the Gulf of Mexico? Would that reaction be any different if those ships remained at an appropriate distance, as prescribed by international law, of any territory under the aegis of the United States (such as Hawaii, Puerto Rico, Guam, etc.) while at the same time China was negotiating with Russia to purchase two nuclear submarines?*

There was a time, mainly during the early and mid-twentieth century, when the United States was the world's greatest producer; now it is the world's greatest consumer. Understandably then, while our supply chain remained stalled due mainly to a lack of transportation, the shelves of a variety of retail stores and shops were, if not bare, scantily stocked for the Christmas holidays. The bulk of our imports were waiting uncertainly on ships offshore and in container parks at our ports. A great number of those imports came from the Far East, mainly from China, but also from Singapore, South Korea, Japan, and Bangladesh. Substantial quantities of imported goods come also from Mexico, Canada, and not least from Europe. Meanwhile, we

---

* China and Russia have held joint military training maneuvers in Siberia at least once already. Can we envision another Bamboo Curtain slowly beginning to come down as one did under Mao Tse Tung's regime? This trenchant question becomes even more evocative now that House Speaker Pelosi has made her goodwill visit to Taiwan.

manufacture such essential items as vehicles and other fossil fueled machines and all manner of fat-fried snacks (Doritos, Fritos, Cheetos, etc.). One TV commercial advertising patio awnings or canopies proudly announces that their products are "Assembled in the U.S.A.!" (but probably manufactured in Mexico, or elsewhere).

A hundred years ago, people all over the world were driving Henry Ford's Model-Ts and taking pictures of one another with George Eastman's Kodak box cameras. Rails were being laid down and bridges and buildings were being constructed using steel from Pittsburgh and Birmingham. And if we hadn't had the capability and will to produce all those tanks and other vehicles, planes, food, medical supplies, virtually all the accoutrements for a world war, and perhaps even more important, provided the money and the men, our allies alone could not have been victorious in two world wars.

Today most of those countries who bought our steel to build them have better railway systems than ours. Admittedly, and as De Tocqueville realized almost two centuries ago, the love of wealth supersedes everything else in this country. Although our freight railways are in much better state than are our passenger carriers, they still are inadequate to deal with the cargo delivery delays we are experiencing now when there aren't enough truckers to deliver the goods, thereby increasing inflation and thus retail prices on virtually everything consumers buy.* And when there are adequate trucks and their drivers again they

---

* Under "normal" conditions, seventy-two percent of all goods in the U.S. are shipped by truck.

will continue to wreak havoc on our roads and bridges. Consider also that Amtrak derailment in Missouri in late May, 2022, at an uncontrolled vehicle crossing. There are 10,000 more such crossings in the country.

Commercial air travel has been a principal factor in the decline of the railroads, especially for the passenger carriers. As Ben Franklin observed, "Time is money," giving more impetus to that overriding love of wealth that obsesses us. Among too many Americans today there is a fretful impatience: "I want it now!"; "I can't wait until…"; "I wish (it or they) would hurry up and (get here, or make up their minds)." I wish that our government were similarly imbued with the importance of time. I have already pointed out some advantages of traveling by sea; going by train has its own benefits, which will become obvious if you give the matter a little thought. Don't take busses unless you have to.

In this discussion of transportation, I've said nothing about POV (privately owned vehicles), which along with those cargo trucks I have mentioned are contributing to the destruction of what is left of a second-rate network of roads and bridges built in the 1950s. When General Eisenhower left his post as Supreme Commander of Allied Forces Europe, he came home with many memories, some good, some bad.* One that had impressed him greatly was Germany's system of *Autobahnen*, Hitler's network of superhighways. At the time of "Ike's" return, all we had to compare with this masterpiece of civil engineering was what we called the Lincoln Highway, or U.S. 1, that ran

---

* We lost more than 4,000 men on Omaha Beach alone on that first long day of the Normandy invasion.

east to west through Pennsylvania, and compared to those *Autobahnen*, looked like a country lane with a plethora of billboards, lunch wagons, filling stations, and cabins along the way.* That would be analogous to comparing a picture by Grandma Moses to a priceless Rembrandt or a spavined old dray horse to Man o' War or his son, War Admiral.

When he was elected President in 1952, Eisenhower lost no time in setting the wheels in motion to emulate that German modern day miracle of engineering.† What supported Eisenhower's efforts in getting the legislation and funding for his dream of an American replica of the German highways was the fact that because of our total commitment to the war effort, no civilian vehicles except for a quantity of 1941 Fords and some less popular vehicles to serve as staff cars were manufactured during the war, as Sherman tanks were coming off Detroit's assembly lines. When the Allied victory was in sight, hundreds of thousands of Americans were putting in their orders for new cars. Today, despite the poor condition of our infrastructure, our roads are literally crawling with POV, like fleas on a poor homeless dog,

---

* For those of you younger readers, a lunch wagon now is a diner, a filling station is a gas or service station, and a cabin is a motel or motor lodge. Foreign friends of mine when visiting our shores have asked why we Americans, living in a country of such natural beauty have such a proclivity for all this garish commercialism. I refer them to that great god Mammon.
† After the Allied invasion at Normandy, when Germany's defeat became more inevitable than probable and the allies had achieved air superiority and then actual supremacy, Adolph Galland, who commanded what was left of the Luftwaffe's fighter arm and was himself a decorated hero, used, for the few aircraft left at his disposal, the Autobahn as runways after our ground forces had occupied or destroyed the airfields he had been able to use earlier.

vehicles of every conceivable kind, with strange–sounding names, even unto one that flies. When I'm in a wistful mood I wish I had that 1932 four-cylinder Ford Model B truck that I learned to drive in.

So when there was a time that China needed our steel to build her railways and her wealthy warlords were driven around in our Model-T Fords, today they have 300 mph bullet trains and make cars with artificially intelligent robots that can engage their human operators in brief practicable dialogue. And today there are qualified sources who are predicting that in the not so distant future we'll be having a "space race" with the Chinese; we're already behind the North Koreans in the development of hypersonic ballistic missiles.

It is true that in the field of aeronautics we lead the world, with the development of microchip technology running not far behind. This may seem an anomaly in view of what has been said already, but there is a reasonable explanation. Wars always advance technology in its myriad forms and fields, and the Second World War was no exception. In all the weapons and machines of ground and naval operations, in field and rear echelon medical requirements, commissary and quartermaster supply, across the entire spectrum of the requirements for waging total war one saw significant advances, quantum leaps forward, even breakthroughs in modern technology, and not least in aeronautics. Boeing continued to turn out improved versions of its B-17 Flying Fortresses, and later the B-29, which was used to obliterate Hiroshima and Nagasaki. Boeing led the way in heavy bombers and didn't stop with the end of the war. I think their B-52 is still in service, celebrating its seventieth birthday. The Air Force had to build a new two-mile runway at their base at Presque Isle, Maine in order to give it an adequate take-off run. The B-52 base at Rome, New York was turned over to civilian uses at the end of the Cold War, but I think there's still a gaggle of the vintage bombers on Guam and another death-dealing flock on Diego Garcia, an island in the Indian Ocean, both ready to carpet bomb some defenseless country somewhere. Cambodians are still trying to clear out the seven million dollars' worth of antipersonnel mines spawned by the cluster bombs we dropped on their rice fields in the latter stages of the Vietnam War near the Angel's Wing and the Parrot's Beak. But enough about that venerable but very useful bearer of death and destruction. During the "Big War" Douglas turned out its B-24, B-25, and B-26 medium bombers, C-46 and C-47 troop-cargo planes (militarized DC-3s); Lockheed built fighters and troop-cargo aircraft such as the C-82 followed by the improved C-119.

The jet engine was a breakthrough, although we cannot take credit for its invention. The Italians flew the first jet airplane at a 1931 airshow, and though its maximum speed was only 150 mph, it was a true jet. The Germans introduced the Messerschmidt-262 to aerial combat too late in the war to do them much good, but that twin-engine fighter opened the door to all future flight (thus far). For reasons that are beyond the scope of this treatise, Douglas left the field of commercial aeronautics with its DC-8, its only jet aircraft after its success with its propeller driven commercial series of the DC-2, 3, 4, 6 and 7. Lockheed has gone on successfully, producing, after those C-82s and C-119s of the 1940s and '50s troop and cargo carriers, the propeller-driven C-23 and C-130, and the jet powered C-141, followed by the huge C-5 and C-5A and now the C-17,* all under contract with our Air Force. Hughes Aircraft Company (mainly rotary wing) and others see to the needs of the rest of the armed forces.

The Chinese communists, having emerged victorious in their civil war against Chiang Kai Shek's Nationalists, did not have the military or naval resources necessary to make their victory complete by invading and occupying the former Japanese island of Formosa, now Taiwan, to which the remainder of the Nationalists had withdrawn and found refuge in after their defeat on the mainland in 1949. Little did the rest of the world realize that Taiwan was to become the prosperous Chinese Nationalist stronghold it is today. The only memorable comment to come out of Washington officialdom was "Well, now we've lost China!" arrogantly, and totally ignoring the fact that China, a sovereign nation under whatever form of governance she chose, and whatever we may have done to help rid them of the Japanese, with whom we ourselves had been at war, was never ours to lose. Nonetheless, mainland China gave some substance to that claim, however arrogant, of our having truly lost her when Chicom troops surged across the Yalu River to join

---

* The C-17 achieved fame, or notoriety, at Kabul Airport when during our hasty and chaotic withdrawal from Afghanistan two young Afghan men, desperate to flee the newly reinstated Taliban, clung to the exterior of the gigantic refugee-packed cargo plane as it took off. When the C-17 reached an altitude of about 200 feet, they could hold on no longer and fell to their deaths. So much for our exalted departure and one of our more recent failures in our amateurish attempts at "nation building."

their North Korean comrades the following year in their war against the ROK (Republic of Korea) and their U.N. allies: the United States and relatively small contingents from eleven other U.N. member nations. Those Chicom reinforcements were instrumental in preventing an outright victory by those U.N. forces and subsequently enabled the North Koreans to negotiate an armistice at the 38th parallel, a treaty that still exists today.

Although her path has not been without problems: "losing" Taiwan, whose population now comprises twenty-four million people; its restrictions on child births (her population now has reached almost one and one-half billion); Mao's cultural revolution; the Tiananmen Square massacre where, according to student leaders, 3,400 civilians were killed; the uprising in Hong Kong; their unquestionable human rights abuses; the dangerous encounters with vessels of our Seventh Fleet in the South China Sea; the trade tariff and COVID-19 contretemps during the Trump administration; despite all that China has performed what might be called a double miracle of governance and economics. Witness the construction of the Three Rivers Dam that is saving untold numbers of lives during the annual flood season. From the birth of the Maoist communist party under the tutelage of Soviet advisors in 1924, and earlier under the titular emperor and the fractional chaos of the warlords, then through the Second World War with its Japanese incursion compelling them to form a united front with the Nationalists, and ultimately to their long-fought struggle for supremacy over Chiang Kai Shek's Koumintang (Nationalist Party) and final victory in 1949, they persevered. And now, after all their difficulties both domestic and international, they must be considered as one of the world's major powers, and given the magnitude of our own disarray presently, rather sooner than later may become a superpower and replace us in our rather tenuous hold on that title.

11

Looking back at history a little, it is of interest at that time of tense uncertainty when the Russians had encircled her border with Ukraine with troops and placed several divisions in Belarus, about what she would do next. It seemed surprising that at such a crucial moment President Putin left the Kremlin to join Chinese President Xi Jingpin for the opening of the Olympics in China. What makes Putin's visit even more interesting is that many if not all notables from other nations did not attend the games in protest of China's human rights transgressions. Relations have been warming between the two nations, especially since China has sided openly with Russia in her demands that NATO and the European Union stop encroaching on her western flank by supporting eastern European nations who wish to be completely independent and separated from Russia's sphere of influence. There also is the matter of those heavy sanctions the U.S. and its European allies can invoke that would seriously impact the Russian economy. The greatest and most lucrative Russian export is that of huge quantities of liquid gas the European states are dependent upon. If Putin can reach an agreement with China about importing Russian gas he would be in a much stronger position to defy the threats from the U.S. and her allies over the Ukraine dispute, and for the matter of that ease the entire controversy over the fate of other states seeking independence in eastern Europe and even elsewhere. Of course, the future impact of House Speaker Pelosi's visit to Taiwan on U.S.-China relations is yet to be revealed.

Mention of the Korean War takes us to, at least in a literary sense, Seoul, capital of South Korea. "Frozen Chosen," as some preferred to call it in those less palmy days during and for years after the Korean War, was a far cry from what it is today. A "bus" going through the dirty and dismal streets of Seoul was constructed of flattened fifty-five-gallon steel fuel drums as its superstructure, with "windows" cut out of them (no glass), all mounted, along with an engine and power train, on the chassis of a two and one-half-ton U.S. Army cargo truck. Domestic stoves used empty beer cans (made of steel in those days*) welded together end to end to serve as flu pipes. We helped by emptying as many full ones as we could find.

It was said then that those South Koreans could make anything out of a tin can; their problem was that they couldn't make a tin can. That's as may be, but the reasons had nothing to do with their intelligence, ingenuity, or industriousness, as is the case with most Asians. The real reasons lie in their suppression by the Japanese who had occupied Korea for forty years after their victory in the Russo-Japanese War in 1905. The Japanese occupiers treated them as serfs, putting them in no position of responsibility or authority in the administration of their own country. This yoke of suppression was followed just a few years after the defeat and departure of the Japanese in 1945 by that devastating Korean War of three years' duration. No; the South Koreans are not deficient in any of the qualities

---

* Giving "beer can crusher" a more impressive meaning than it has now.

required for true nation building. All they needed was the opportunity to display those qualities. I could suggest that you visit there now, so you could witness a prime example of a socio-political example of progress made under the bleakest if not the direst conditions.

Aside from the material aspects of this progress made by China and South Korea is the preeminent matter of ideologies. While China has evolved (devolved might be a better word) into a system of governance that could be called capitalistic socialism, with occasional echoes of authoritarian, and even dictatorial communism (but without Mao's despotic rigidity), the South Koreans have achieved a socio-capitalistic democracy. When I first was in Korea there were two hotels in Seoul: The Chosen Hotel, which became our officer's Club, and the Bando Hotel, which was owned outright by President Sygman Rhee's Austrian wife, Donna Maria, who also owned that tin-can bus company I described. The communists in the North weren't the only problem the South Koreans had in those days.

Former President Trump's inept, self-seeking, and in some cases farcical attempts in the conduct of foreign relations have been reported by reliable sources and recorded by honest historians and political scientists. Unfortunately, even tragically, tens of millions of people in America, who seem to be under some spell of enchantment cast by this demagogue, refuse to accept the truth. Donald J. Trump is a paranoidal narcissist and has been one since his boyhood, when he probably hid his own Easter eggs (he still does, metaphorically). As President, the highest elective position in the nation, he had some cover for his sociopathic pronouncements and actions, but now, ostensibly as a civilian and subject to the same laws and restrictions as any other citizen (aside from such undeserved perquisites as secret service security and a library, although I can't see any reason he should need or want one), now he is somehow still in a position of authority, informal as it may be, over those seventy-five or eighty million voters whom he holds in thrall. The harm he has done and continues to do to our already frail democracy is incalculable. It must be left to historians to judge and report years from now, assuming those historians along with the rest of us survive the ravages of climate change. Perhaps more important than his misguided public support is the proven fact that he controls, again however indirectly, the great majority of Republicans in the Congress, either because they want to retain their seats of power, or they are merely more of those true acolytes who have come to believe in this latter-day political Messiah without portfolio. This somewhat digressive prelude takes us to the Peoples Republic of Korea (PRK), a place our traveler should avoid unless he has a very compelling reason to go there. As for me, I don't think I would learn anything more than I already know for my purpose in writing about it.

Trump's brief one-sided love affair with Kim Jong-Un, President of the PRK, was fruitless and made us a laughing stock in diplomatic circles around the world. When this theatre of the absurd ended, the North Koreans went blithely on, without any restraint on the development of improved delivery systems for their stockpile of NBC (nuclear, biological, and chemical) weapons. Recently, and as I've already mentioned, they have developed a series of hypersonic ballistic missiles, each in the series more powerful than its predecessor, that puts them in the Mach 5, or some claim even the Mach 10 range (five to ten times the speed of sound). Even our own research and development experts admit that these outperform any delivery means we now have available, and that we haven't the means to defend against it. In mid-January 2022, the North Koreans launched two of their hypersonic missiles, causing our FAA (Federal Aviation Administration) to "ground stop" all commercial flights on our West Coast.

During Trump's showy and amateurish exercise in futility and his mainly unrequited love affair with Kim Jon-Un, China remained silent but observant. That same China, admittedly rigidly communistic at the time, sent hordes of its soldiers across the Yalu River to aid the North Koreans in 1950. Although there seems to be no connection between China and the PRK's advances in missilery, the news outlets allege that "we are in a space race with China." In any case, it seems to me that there is little reason to send indigenous agents across the 38th parallel to spy on the North Koreans.* Today, they seem pleased to announce their advances in certain weaponry openly and even proudly, quite probably part of a strategic psyops plan, the objective(s) of which I can only guess at. Should the North, in their fervor to occupy the entire peninsula come down like wolves upon the flock once again with their legions of troops however, even though the Chinese do not interfere to assist

---

* In the days when Kim Jong-Un's grandfather, Kim Il Sung, was the President of the PRK, and before the "spy in the sky" satellites replaced much of that kind of information gathering.

them this time, our assurances to defend the South Koreans will have little meaning with the 28,500 troops we have stationed there. Unless we sent massive reinforcements there in time, they, along with their ROK (Republic of Korea) counterparts would be the first to be killed, wounded, or taken prisoner. We must ask ourselves: would this end in another disastrous, disgraceful departure by the leader of the free world?

In the late 1940s George Kennan, advocate of the Containment Theory, a means of impeding the spread of communism, said that the United States must always have an enemy, even if it has to invent one. He could have made that "enemies," since in our case today though it may be highly improbable it is not impossible, especially in these times of domestic turmoil and seemingly endless partisanship and in the midst of a continuing pandemic, not inconceivable that we could be confronted by a hostile coalition that sets out to destroy us. The composition of such a coalition? Economics would play a significant part in such a scenario, unless we were completely occupied by a foreign force, or if nuclear weapons of strategic power were employed, making economics irrelevant throughout what is left of our world (in the Cold War it was called MAD, mutually assured destruction). For those of you who may be wondering which candidates might be willing to join such an overwhelming coalition, consider these: China, Russia, North Korea, Iran, Iraq, Afghanistan, and possibly even Pakistan.

12

With due deference to the leaders and foreign service officers who hate to apologize almost as much as they do being caught in a lie, I have this to say. These people are grounded in the use of circumlocution, diversion, broad mental reservations, begging the question, and other epistemological devices to mask the lie of the moment or an egregious act or costly error. Donald Trump is a classic example, though probably self-trained. They become inured to any feelings of guilt about such unethical and immoral practices. They see their deceptions as merely a matter of pragmatism, whether it is in their own interest or some other cause, one too often that it doesn't serve the common good. In short, if it works to achieve your ends, use it.

Did anyone in official U.S. channels apologize, publicly, for the killing of two to three million Southeast Asian citizens, most of whom were only guilty of just being there, during the Vietnam War? Somehow we Americans have become indifferent to common societal decencies. It has become commonplace to answer insouciantly a question such as "But why did you promise me you would never do that again?" with "I lied," as if that should be a perfectly reasonable and adequate answer. Truth and mendacity seem to have become bedfellows and not hostile or even strangers to one another at all. In fact, lying seems to be achieving an equal status with honesty. With so many lies being told us today, not least by the Government, we have "whistle blower aids" now. W.C. Fields' "You can't cheat an honest man" has lost its prudential potency, so there must be many more people getting bilked out there now.*

Mention of Fields' name brings to mind another Hollywood celebrity who had a word of advice for his vast audience, which was composed in great part by young American boys. John Wayne, a classic homespun American hero who seldom sought a non-violent end to problems encountered in his film rôles, once admonished a junior officer with this stern dictum: "Don't ever apologize, Mister: it's a sign of weakness!" Attila the Hun, yes, perhaps to his sons; but to millions of American boys in their formative years? It doesn't matter who wrote the screenplay, or the book from which it was adapted, nor even whoever supplied the additional dialogue; what matters is that John Wayne said it. John Wayne! So it must be true. I don't think so.† I prefer the advice give me by a favorite uncle: "Remember, a gentleman is never unintentionally rude."

There is at least one benefit of traveling by map rather than by air, sea, or other of the usual means of ground transport, and that is time. What would take hours, days, or in some cases even weeks, takes minutes or just seconds if one goes by maps or a terrestrial globe. Still, sometimes I

---

* As I've written elsewhere, this is the day of "Anything Goes" and "I'm Okay, You're Okay," with anti-heroes portrayed by actors such as Dustin Hoffman, Richard Dreyfuss and Woody Allen replacing such matinée idols as Cary Grant, Clark Gable, or Randolph Scott. Similarly, revisionist films such as *The Getaway* or *In Bad Company* portray thieves and other criminals as worthy, even admirable people. Everywhere today (not least in politics) crime does seem to pay.

† Unless he was out hunting or target shooting, John Wayne never heard a live round fired, especially one fired in anger. The movie in which he made that spurious dictum was *She Wore A Yellow Ribbon*.

wish there were those old British P&O (Pacific and Orient) passenger ships in service, with their (mainly) genial crews and passengers, and the people Somerset Maugham met and wrote about in his short stories at various ports of call in that exotic East. Having seen that Japan lies to the southeast of the Korean peninsula at a distance of about 600 miles was the work of less than a minute for our traveler when he found the proper page in his atlas.

Although we may remember Pearl Harbor, where about 3,000 of our servicemen and a number of civilians were killed in the Japanese attack there on December 7th, 1941, the Japanese remember Hiroshima and Nagasaki which were literally obliterated in early August of 1945 with hundreds of thousands of Japanese civilians killed. Some, who haven't succumbed to old age, still are dying as a result of the deadly radiation spewed by "Fat Boy" or "Little Albert" or whatever quaint names were given those 20 kiloton bombs detonated 1500 feet above those cities.

Some will tell you that those attacks were merely tests of the efficacy of what then were "atomic bombs"; others that they were used to end the war before we had to invade the Japanese home islands, thus sustaining what undoubtedly would be very heavy casualties inflicted on our side; while still others held that it was simply revenge for what the Japanese had done at Pearl Harbor, Hickham and Wheeler Fields, adding "Hell, it wasn't any worse than what Churchill and "Bomber" Harris did with their 10,000 pound blockbusters to Hamburg and Dresden!" Years later, some even more calloused wags were joking that those horrendous events were as nothing compared to the thirty-some McDonalds we had established in Tokyo.

In her halcyon days of the early 1980s, Japan became one of our most important creditors. Japan, whose cheap, flimsy toys such as kewpie dolls, pinwheels, or other gimcracks were given as prizes in games of chance at carnivals, amusement parks, boardwalk stands, or other fêtes, became the butt of jokes for any next to worthless object of any intended use during the years prior to World War II. After the war and when Japan began producing such breakthrough items as transistor radios with printed circuits and other exports, they no longer evoked derisive comments. Rather, those products were highly praised and marketed throughout the world. Incidentally, in the 1930s, when we accepted their gimcracks and scorned them and any other product "made in Japan" and at the same time refused to sell oil to them, we were providing a major reason for their making war on us. Although economic sanctions often are ineffectual there are times when they have unintended and adverse consequences, to include a *casus belli*. Consider President Biden's threats against Russia's Nord Stream 2 gas pipeline to western Europe and President Putin's trip to China to attend the opening of the Winter Olympics. If China agrees to replace the European market for gas supply from Russia that could just draw the teeth from Biden's threat. However that situation turns out we'll still have to raise our debt ceiling since we already aren't even able to pay the interest on the debts we have now.

We presently maintain 53,700 troops in Japan. Are these to help defend Japan from a possible attack (from whom?)

or to serve as an advanced base, as we did with England in preparation for the Normandy invasion, in the event that North Korea invades South Korea again?

As much as our traveler might have enjoyed a ten day or two-week sea voyage to Australia, news about events back in the States have made him decide that he should return there without further delay. Unrest in Canada, our closest ally geographically, about mandates and strictures caused by the COVID-19 pandemic that were beginning to reflect those in the U.S. bolstered his decision, as well as the intensifying situation in eastern Europe. His intention of going to an antipodal country had been to look into Australia's position on political and military matters in the Southeast Asian region and more particularly on that nuclear submarine negotiation with the U.S. which so angered the French. He had also considered a side trip to Antarctica, but decided that all to be gained there would be confirmation that the Ross Ice Shelf was disappearing into the sea.

Our globe trotter is flying back, and while he is in the air I will recall those pleasantries I so enjoyed dining at Suehiro's restaurant, the Grande Sante bath house, Watanabe's band, (which sounded exactly like Glenn Miller's), and those wonderful "stand up" Tempura bars along the streets when I lived for a time in Tokyo's Shibuya-ku (district).

13

Now that our traveler is home and once again engaged in his own affairs I'll ask you to recall what I have written about a possible civil war, or revolution, or some other attempted *coup d'état*. The last of these seems most likely if there is to be any uprising at all. To think that none of these could possibly be contemplated, let alone occur, would be to ignore that old but still sound adage, "'tis better to be safe than sorry."

The assured loyalty of all our armed forces would be crucial in such an eventuality. Months ago, three retired U.S. generals composed and released to the *New York Times* a letter expressing their "bone chilling fears" about the potential threat of the loyalty of our armed forces to the existing Federal government should a *coup* be attempted. What they were saying and feared would make the 1/6 incident look like a walk in the park by comparison. During an interview on CNN one of these officers claimed that 124 U.S. officers (on active duty, one presumes) already were in league with the dissidents, and that a lieutenant general had actually called for such a *coup* to take place.

If our armed forces haven't been surveyed and satisfactorily vetted, and I am certain that they haven't been, we should do so immediately, without those needless delays with which our government, at every level, is ridden. Such a procedure should be placed on a wartime footing, as were all Federal projects during World War II. Since we are in a war with the pandemic, as has been said so many times, we are in no state to fight another simultaneously, and certainly not one within the precincts of our own country. Such an investigation must include all State National Guard and Reserve units of all the services in our armed forces and all law enforcement officers at or below the Federal level. The FBI, after proper vetting of its own thousands of personnel, should then devote themselves to the greater task. Now I can almost hear a reader who knows a little Latin asking himself: *quis custodiet ipsos custodes?* (who will guard the guards themselves?). Less elegantly put are those old homilies: "sending the fox to guard the henhouse" or "the wolf to guard the sheep." Well, if there aren't enough right-thinking loyal Americans left to do the job properly and honestly, why don't we just throw up our hands and accept whatever horrors we may be in for? That may sound somewhat feeble as an answer to the problem, but after having given the matter a good deal of thought it's all I've got to offer. But remember also what I said about not being able to make a good pot out of poor clay.

If our foresight had been as keen as our hindsight not long into Trump's presidency, and our legislators had been truly dedicated to the public's welfare, we could have found a way to carry out such an onerous but essential enterprise. The Republicans in the Senate bear the major part of the blame, however indirectly. After all, the House impeached Trump twice during his first term in office, an action unprecedented in presidential history, but the Senate refused to convict him on both occasions. If Joe McCarthy could see his way for his ill-informed, misbegotten, and yes, ignorant reasons for his "investigation" almost three quarters of a century ago, could we not strive at least as hard to save what is left of our democracy? I can envision a number of eyebrows being raised when reading what I have suggested. The amount of work involved, the time it would consume…. What then, if it isn't to work, are those two million Federal employees paid to do?

I think a little clarification would be helpful here, so I'll give you a homespun analogy. In the days before steam powered sawmills, logs had to be split by hand to provide more finished lumber for construction. Wedges and single-bladed axes or sledge hammers were used to do the splitting, by a man who knew how to split logs. Now imagine that we, the people, are that big, solid, and with a few knots and other minor imperfections, straight and symmetrical log. And now here comes a man with an axe or a heavy hammer and enough sharp wedges to split that tough and stately log. That man is not "Honest Abe" from Illinois, but Donald J. Trump. I think you see my point. In every country or society, sooner or later, a "Trump" appears, but fortunately for that country or society in most cases he doesn't have the wealth or power (and in this country wealth is power) or whatever else it takes to influence people and so has no significance. But if he has money and therefore some power and is not clever but cunning, he can emerge from the depths of insignificance to achieve a position of prominence. Add to this his manipulative abilities and absolute amorality and you have a Trump.* These are perilous, if not desperate, times in great part due to the partisanship instigated and

---

* If I combined two very old English metaphors I would describe Trump as a "sly boots" driving a "slow coach" (his followers).

now perpetuated by Trump and his seemingly spellbound malefactors. Some logs should never be split, but reserved for the more foundational parts of construction.

As least for this citizen, Christmas past was a rather quiet and private affair, thanks mainly to this ever-present pandemic. There was a time, perhaps a half-century ago, and without the limitations and restrictions necessary to ward off the virus, when we would see the "word" XMAS or Xmas here and there, on gift-wrapped packages, greeting cards, or elsewhere at that time of year. Today, if such a word is still in use, I haven't seen it, and if political correctness was responsible for its demise you can score a point for Donna Shalala (who coined the name for the pestilential practice) and her adherents. There remains the fact that the original meaning and reason for the celebratory holiday was the birth of Christ. Although the actual date of the event may have differed, the 25th of December was settled upon as the day of the blessed event. After Xmas left the scene one began to find it difficult to find a greeting card that contained the word "Christmas"; virtually all cards sent or received wished one "Season's" or "Holiday" greetings. At the same time we began to hear about Hanukkah, a Jewish celebration of the consecration of a Hebrew temple of ancient times, accompanied one year by the Empire State Building becoming resplendent in blue and white lights (Israel's national colors). About the same time, in late December, and not to be outdone, we also were introduced to the African Kwanza celebration, about which I still know nothing. What I did realize was that the greatest celebration of someone's birth in the world of Christendom was being infringed upon by other religious sects as well as with the commercial interests it has been saddled with and battened upon from time immemorial. Since that is the case, we may as well rededicate it to Santa Claus and rename it Crixnix, which would be no worse than Xmas and at the same time descriptive of our desecration. Crixnix, if we were to invoke a little schmalzy German, could be a contraction of sorts of *Christus Nichts*, which translated would mean Christ nothing or naught. So for that day yet to come, assuming we all survive that long, I wish you all a Happy Crixnix!

14

B ut as much as I enjoy a little levity occasionally, I must go on with more serious matters as we ramble along. Since Americans are so captivated by simple rhymes—Jesus is the reason for the season (in keeping with what I was just talking about), and Keep your eyes on the prize! and even more with alliteration, I'll see what I can do, at least with the latter. As we continue our stroll I won't take you to the Boulevard of Broken Dreams on which is situated the Heartbreak Hotel, a place I don't recommend but where necessity required me to stay on a few occasions; but there are other places of equal or even more interest to visit as we go along. Of these I suggest that we turn our steps to Pandemic Plaza to begin with, and then in turn to Armalite Alley, Addicts Avenue, Portly Place, and Racial Road. There will be those of you who already have some personal knowledge of what we will see and hear, and perhaps they can help to enlighten those of you who have not as we go along.

The COVID-19 pandemic, or more precisely the way that we have dealt with it for almost three years, suggests the more ominous word, pandemonium. As I've noted elsewhere, although the death rate has dropped from 2500 to 1000 deaths per day, the overall total has passed the million mark. Dr. Birx, one of former President Trump's medical advisors, has alleged that as many as 130,000 lives could have been saved were it not for the Trump administration's ineptitude. Other experts have said that as few as 20,000 would have died if the required mitigation actions had been imposed* (testing, masking, quarantine, tracing, and social distancing) instead of Trump's bland assurances and ridiculous suggestions for treatment. Now, despite the fact that it has been proven conclusively that the vaccines are the only real assurance that we can keep this plague at bay, only about sixty percent of the population has had its basic inoculations, while it is of equal or more importance that only twenty-five percent have had the necessary booster shots. This now is of even more importance since new variants are superseding the Omicron strain; the available vaccines can control them even though they are even more transmissible than Omicron.†

More than ninety percent of those who are dying from the COVID-19 virus had not been vaccinated, and as I've said before, and though it may seem insensitive, except for those relatively few with *valid* medical or religious reasons, I won't mourn for the rest. I *will* mourn for the victims of those wrong-headed, ignorant, and indifferent imbeciles who infected them unnecessarily. Those antimandate truckers in Canada and their American counterparts in the Windsor-Detroit area and elsewhere along the U.S.-Canadian border didn't help matters at all, especially as delays in the supply chain continued to boost inflation.

---

* Why Trump and his collaborators have not been indicted for facilitating genocidal murder is something I will never understand or countenance.

† More recently, we've had to endure the B-1 variant, followed by the B-5 variant, the most transmissible variant yet, and at the same time a virus known as Monkey Pox; we now have an eighth of all the cases reported worldwide of the latter disease, for which we have inadequate supplies of vaccine. Much like the AIDS epidemic in the 1980s, more than ninety percent of reported cases are among gay men. Same sex marriage, anyone?

Let us move along to Armalite Alley (named for the Colt AR-15, a favorite weapon of our mass murderers). As with the pandemic, the death toll in the shooting of innocent civilians has reached staggering heights. The major cities in the U.S. have broken homicide records during this year while nothing substantive has been done to stop the ever increasing carnage. There is one way to stop the problem, and that is to eliminate or to at least strictly control the use of the weapons used in this runaway and ceaseless slaughter in which so many of the victims are innocent children. Soon, CNN may be announcing daily: "And now here is the mass shooting report for the last twenty-four hours…."

Forty-five percent of all firearms in the possession of civilians in the world exists here, in the U.S. Since the Columbine shooting, 320 children have been killed in shootings. The Governor of Texas does nothing about mass shootings but is adamantly opposed to abortion for any reason; he's selective in the mode of killing humans. Since 2020, the number one killer of children is no longer auto accidents, it's guns. In the first 147 days of 2020, there were 315 deaths by shootings. There have been 500 school shootings since 2008. As of July 4th, 2022, there were 309 mass shootings (four or more victims) and 275 gunshot deaths in this country. In sum, with about four percent of the world's population, barring our armed forces and law enforcement agencies, we have eight times the number of killings than Canada (which has recently banned all pistols and assault rifles); fifty times those in Germany; 100 times those in England; and 250 times those in Japan*, to list only four *civilized* nations. President Biden should declare a nationwide emergency and nationalize the entire arms and ammunition industry.

The shooting at the Tops Market in Buffalo on May 14th, 2022, followed ten days later by the Robb Elementary School abomination at Uvalde, Texas, combined with incidental shootings during the intervening weekend here and there totaled 108 dead and 365 wounded. Let us take a closer look at that grisly and shocking incident at Uvalde. The continued obfuscation and outright lying by all the law enforcement personnel involved in responding to the shooting, all were grounded in and stemming from their ineptitude and even more, their craven cowardice in the face of danger to themselves. If ever placed in the hands of our shameful judicial system, they will never be held fully accountable for the unnecessary deaths of most of the victims.

Once the shooter had been "neutralized,"† the scene in the two classrooms where the students met their horrid fate, the eldest ones aged about ten years, was ghastly beyond

---

* In 2021 there were 45,034 shooting deaths in the U.S. and one in Japan. In 2022 there was one more in Japan in which former Prime Minister Shinzo Abe was shot to death by a man using a homemade gun.

† By the time that "active shooter" himself was shot dead, there were 376 law enforcement "heroes" from twenty agencies on the scene. Based upon past police responses to such encounters, that eighteen-year-old murderer must have had more holes in his body than a colander. That leaked seventy-seven minutes of film of those cowardly responders showed one craven weakling coolly reaching for a hand sanitizer while hearing those innocents being slaughtered. Ask yourselves: what would true justice demand in such a case?

description. Those unacquainted with violent death would have witnessed something shocking and even beyond their belief. They would have seen small, headless corpses, others literally torn apart, some eviscerated, with their small organs and entrails lying next to them, gouts of blood spattered everywhere, with their semi-sweet smell assailing their nostrils. In short, they would find themselves in a veritable shambles, an abattoir of small human bodies or their parts. In clearing out this charnel house, the coroner's or medical examiner's task would be an unenviable and daunting one. Since small children seldom carry any identification, in some cases a child's clothing was used to identify the victim, in others, with the cooperation of grieving parents, DNA had to be resorted to.

The eighteen-year-old shooter's choice of weapons was one of twenty varieties of the Colt Armalite, commonly called the AR-15, a civilian equivalent of the military M-16; not as good an all-around weapon as Kalashnikov's AK-47 perhaps, but still, in at least one model, a high-powered weapon with a muzzle velocity of 4200 feet per second. It would seem to those whose knowledge of ballistics is rudimentary that the AR-15's .223 caliber projectile is little more than that of the .22 caliber bullet of the "plinking" or target rifle, given to twelve-year-old boys in rural areas to teach them how to hunt by shooting squirrels or rabbits or other "varmints," but anyone who has a basic knowledge of small arms and sees the cartridges used in each weapon sees the difference immediately. The jacketed projectile in a .223 round is mounted in a shouldered cartridge case that contains a much greater charge than the .22 short or even long cartridge (the shooting galleries of yore used .22 rim fire shorts).

According to military ballistics standards, it takes fifty-three foot-pounds of terminal kinetic energy to disable the average soldier (five feet eight inches tall and weighing about 150 pounds). In the musket, a .50 caliber ball could disable at sixty yards, but an AR-15 .223 bullet, because of its terminal velocity, can do it at 400 meters (the weapon's maximum effective range). But there is more. That bullet from an Armalite can cause irreparable, hideous damage to a human body, the kind of damage that would make a mortician almost insist that the mourners at any "viewing" would see only a closed casket. When a copper-jacketed bullet at point blank range and travelling at hypersonic speed strikes a human body, the result is almost unimaginable, especially in the case of a small, young, human body. If it finds no obstruction, however slight, it may pass right through, although it will leave an exit wound many times the size of its entry wound. If it strikes any obstruction, a bone or even more dense tissue, it will begin to tumble, causing the shredding of more tissue and even cavitation, a virtual hollowing out of the thorax or abdomen; head shots can cause actual decapitation. In my view, especially in such cases as those of Uvalde and Sandy Hook, open casket viewings should be held, special ones, for all those Congressmen, Governors, and State legislators who have their hands deep in the pockets of and are held in thrall by the gun lobbyists, their indifferent adherents and all those self-seeking yahoos who persist in misinterpreting that antiquated and now literally murderous Second Amendment to the Constitution.* If there were any true Justice in this country, it would be they who were shot to bits. If that seems too extreme, then at the very least they should be tried and convicted of facilitating and contributing to mass murder and sentenced to imprisonment for life. As courage takes different forms, so too does cowardice. Those responders at Uvalde displayed, blatantly, physical cowardess; those in Congress and State capitals continue to exhibit the self-centered moral variety. The lack of physical courage may have tragic results in certain incidents; the lack of moral courage in our Government has a nationwide lethality.

How in good conscience can we consider ourselves a civilized nation while we permit this abomination to continue? I have written extensively about this disgraceful state of affairs, now shameful on an international level, and I have suggested a possible solution, since we won't get any help from Wayne LaPierre (President of the National Rifle Association) or his accomplices in Congress; yes, accomplices, co-conspirators in felony murder if not outright

---

* With the exception of the Eighth Amendment (no excessive bail or fines-17 words) the Second Amendment, with 27, is the shortest in the Bill of Rights and reads: A well-regulated Militia, being necessary to the security of a free State, the right of the people to keep and bear arms, shall not be infringed. The framers, however well-intended, were not grammarians. Those three commas not only were unnecessary, they are at the heart of today's loose and controversial misrepresentation of that all too brief injunction. Read straight through, without any hesitation, that capitalized word "Militia" becomes more prominent and meaningful. As I have said elsewhere, that Amendment was insisted upon by the leaders of those newly free colonies as a safeguard for their rights in the event of any Federal encroachment or infringement on those rights. As I've said also, in those days (1791) a muzzle-loading musket was a far cry from a multimagazined AR-15.

genocide, much like Trump and those avoidable hundreds of thousands of deaths to COVID-19 he caused, however indirectly, while he was in office.

There is only one way to solve or greatly mitigate this sub-epidemic and that is, if we cannot rid ourselves of the weapons used at least we can render the majority of them harmless. Since some things are worthy of repeating, I'll state my suggestion briefly once again. As even the best cameras are useless without film, so too are firearms without ammunition. To the satisfaction of small arms dealers and manufacturers worldwide there are more firearms in the hands of civilians in this country than there are people. To collect, confiscate, or even buy them by the Federal government would be next to impossible, especially with that controversial but now mainly lethal Second Amendment to the Constitution as it now stands, and State's rights, given the fact that the majority of gun owners are honest law abiding citizens. That Second Amendment, much like the Fourteenth and the Ninth in the abortion controversy, provides justification, along with a number of other doctrinal matters, for a Constitutional Convention to review and clarify that foundational document and bring it into consonance with our contemporary legal requirements. But to sum this up, the only feasible solution to our problem in the misuse of firearms and its bloody consequences is to control, rigidly, the availability of ammunition, with appropriate provision for the armed forces and law enforcement.

Let's pause awhile in our ramble, find a park bench, and reflect a little on some incidental matters pertaining to the places we have been visiting and the problems, as I see them, they have been enduring.

*   *   *

I find that I cannot go on with this without inserting another interim note. I now have been working on this book for more than a year and I am in the process of re-editing almost daily. From the book's very beginning, due mainly to the frequent and rapidly changing events in the crises we continue to face and to our own timidity, ineptitude, and indifference, which requires rewriting and lengthy insertions: updating statistics on drug deaths, COVID-19 cases, mass shootings and their fatalities, rising inflationary prices, our failed supply chain issues, abortion rights, deaths and destruction due to climate change, the exponential rise in suicides, all this and more happening with bewildering frequency. Now, lest we become too complacent, we and twenty or more other nations are being introduced to another viral plague called Monkey Pox. Add to all that the geopolitical uncertainty and downright unreliability of other nations on where they stand in the swirl of international political and economic positions, driven mainly by the acquisition of power and wealth at the highest realms of governance.

The double outrage at Uvalde, Texas on the 24th of May 2022 stopped me in my tracks. Vice President Harris's tearful but smiling platitudinous remarks about the slaughter in Buffalo just days earlier did nothing to move me. President Biden went to Uvalde and undoubtedly had a good cry with the families of the toddlers who were shot to bits there, a number of whom could only be identified by their DNA because they were unrecognizable. The result, as always: our "representative" government will remain stalled, wrangling over these latest horrors until memory begins to fade as it always has, and the rest of the world continues to see us as some dithering, retarded, giant child with a peculiarly lethal obsession for killing one another *en masse*, while the merchants of death, battening upon that obsession, continue to fill their pockets with the profits accruing from what clearly is a form of "legalized genocide," all abetted by their criminal co-conspirators on Wall Street, in Washington, and their cohorts in the State capitols.* Added to all this is the soaring suicide rate, often including the mass murderers themselves. One wonders: are we Americans all going collectively insane? I have written to the President, the Governor of my State, and to others in positions of authority. In those letters, I suggested that if we can't control the guns, especially those intended to kill on the battlefield, then we should control the ammunition, using the analogy that as having the best camera but no film renders that machine useless, a firearm with no ammunition is similarly impotent. After one year, and after demanding a reply from the White House Communications Director, I received a letter signed by the President, full of the same platitudinous blather one hears on the news outlets, but without any reference to the suggestion I cited above. I haven't received a reply from anyone else. Meanwhile body armor and AR-15s are selling like hot cakes, as are sixty-round magazines to hold that .223 cal. (or 5.56 mm) ammunition for the many varieties

---

* Firearms manufacturers have made 100 billion dollars in profits in the last ten years as gun violence exploded.

of Armalite 15s. There are forty million AR-15s in civilian hands in this country and there are 100 companies globally that manufacture some version of this weapon. Biden's innocuous reply seemed to support what I've said about collective insanity, with its references to mental background checks. He should be working to nationalize the arms and ammunition industry in this country instead of merely commiserating with the victims' families and loved ones.

To discover that our Constitution has no provision to hold our law enforcement agencies or their agents responsible, legally, for the safety or protection of our citizens brought me to the verge of burning the entire final manuscript of this book.* In Texas, this abridgement of justice is supplemented by State laws that make accountability virtually impossible. If this book and others I have written survive, you can count the number of times I have literally pled for a Constitutional Convention to clarify and to amend certain provisions in that 220 year-old document whose tenets in many cases have become obsolete or at least obsolescent. As to that misinterpreted Second Amendment, in the days of the Founding Fathers the only "long guns" were muzzle-fed muskets or fowling pieces (shotguns). The Amendment's intention was to enable States to maintain their militias (today's National Guard units) to ensure themselves against over-control by the Federal government.

Somewhat reluctantly now, I'll go back to the main text of this dismal treatise.

*   *   *

____

* A dozen drafts preceded the final manuscript.

15

As a general comment applying to all of us in these difficult times is the ironical, irreconcilable difference between the reports of current events, which are almost exclusively disappointing, even grim or worse, and the inevitable and ubiquitous commercials which are in great part lighthearted, often comical, and even ridiculous portrayals of life as the sponsors would have you live it if only if you would buy their products*. There is not a thought or a word about the ominous threats that confront us. One thinks of the two-faced Roman god Janus, with one face smiling and the other frowning, or for those of you who prefer today's somewhat mysterious parlance, the "emoji" (smiling face, frowning face).

A personal objection I have to the broad spectrum of advertising on TV is the exploitation of children, most especially those pathetic victims of disease, accident, or genetic birth defects who tell us with pathetic cheerfulness that thanks to our donations and contributions that they can do virtually anything a normal child can do. As only one revolting example a little legless girl tells us that now, she can run (!). As to those film clips of wretched homeless pets pleading for help and talking animals behaving like humans,

---

* In a Life Alert advertisement, an elderly woman lying on the floor cries out: "I've fallen and I can't get up!" Cut to a fully equipped large fire truck leaving a firehouse on its way to assist her. A half-million dollars of taxpayer money, when a boy on a bicycle could do the job. There were two men in the cab of the fire truck.

I'll leave that to you. I'd rather watch a rat race. And don't miss that children's "symphonic" orchestra performing their rendition of a movement from "Thus Spake Zarathustra," off-key, that would make Richard Strauss writhe in his grave, or the tinny-voiced imitator of the late Mr. Rogers singing, again off key, as did Rogers, some drivel about the product he is promoting. Objective: money. Anything goes in pursuit of wealth.

A little earlier I stated that the majority of Americans, about sixty percent, have been vaccinated with the basic COVID-19 shots but only twenty-five percent have gotten that essential booster shot, with perhaps another to follow. The COVID-19 virus, as in the case of the common cold, may be with us forevermore and may require periodic vaccinations. We have not returned to "normal life" and perhaps we never will, and yet those floating hotels called cruise ships are operating again. Several of these seagoing cattle cars already have been turned away from ports of call they may have planned to visit, and we hear that the airlines are struggling due to the cancellation of thousands of flights that in turn have been caused by so many of their employees calling in sick.

With nine million people worldwide dead of starvation in 2021 and more than a million Americans who died of COVID-19 due to ineptitude, indifference, and plain stupidity in the last few years, CNN continues to outdo itself with presentations such as Stanley Tucci eating his way through Italy and someone named Carlton McCoy, "the Nomad," doing the same here and there through countries far and wide, while infants here in America and throughout the rest of the world are suffering, being hospitalized, and probably dying due to the unforgiveable lack of nourishment they need.

A note about my comments concerning Christmas. If it hasn't regained its rightful throne in season, at least it came in sight of it again as I noticed this Christmas past. TV commentators and their guests greeted each other with "Merry Christmas and Happy Holidays" which is a step in the right direction, or at the very least covers all the bases.

As for President Biden's unscripted, powerful, and subsequently controversial ending of his speech at Warsaw in late March, 2022: "For God's sake, Putin should not remain in power!" I find the excessive press reaction and amount of attention given it, citing the implication of "regime change," utter nonsense. What is so sacrosanct about any regime as to deny anyone the right to say it should be changed? Is there anything in international law that protects such dictators, tyrants, or despots as Hitler, Mussolini, Stalin, Ivan the Terrible, Genghis Khan, Nero, or Vlad the Impaler and yes, Putin, who sees himself contrarily as Peter the Great?

In keeping with the continuing impasse about clearing the air of Russian aircraft (a no-fly zone) over Ukraine, as the Ukrainians have been begging for, it might prove more fruitful to examine international law as it pertains to aerial domain, as it does with maritime law and its offshore limits and marginal waters. I think you may find that the air above her terrestrial boundaries, from the ground into infinity, is under Ukraine's jurisdiction, as is the case with any other sovereign nation.

16

There is one more matter I would like to discuss before leaving the doubtful comforts of this park bench, and it concerns the matter of classified documents. There seems to be a good deal of confusion and controversy about Trump and his handling of classified documents in the latter days of and even after his term as President. Perhaps I can provide some clarification on the subject of classified material in general. Documents alone are not the only objects of classification for security or other reasons, but since they are the objects of concern here, I'll restrict my comments to those as the most common to be classified.

There are three main types of documents that are classified based upon content derivation, the concurrence of the authors' superiors, and based upon their importance and sensitivity: "Confidential," "Secret," and "Top Secret"; we could add a fourth, "Restricted," that is applied to certain Field and other Manuals and is considered meaningless by many in the armed forces. One problematic flaw in the system is our tendency to over-classify documents; another is the existence and availability of copying machines and computer printers. At the highest end of the spectrum are certain documents, mainly of Top Secret rank, that require an esoteric "need to know," or "your eyes only" for access to the information they contain.

Keeping with the specific subject at hand, Trump and his alleged malfeasance, let's stay with the main classification of government documents. All classified documents are required, in their storage and handling, to have distinctive cover sheets. Those cover sheets contain the degree of classification in bold print and broad borders in three different colors: blue for Confidential, red for Secret, and yellow for Top Secret. When not in secure storage they must be signed out by an authorized official with the proper security clearance for access to its contents. It can be modified, or even declassified, or if it is no longer of use or has been superseded or OBE (overtaken by events) it can be destroyed by burning, with a witness in attendance if it is Top Secret, and a certificate of destruction made and filed. No one, to include civilians no matter how high their rank, are authorized to take any classified documents home or anywhere away from their place(s) of official use or storage. Loss, or much more important, misappropriation for any reason or purpose is grounds for severe punishment, and in times of war can be considered an act of treason which could result in one's execution if he or she is found guilty (you may recall the Rosenbergs during the development of the "A-bomb").

As I've said, there still are three main categories of classified documents, with the highest of these Top Secret. For twenty years of active service, I held a Top Secret clearance. I am thankful that I never needed a TSSCI (Top Secret Sensitive Compartmented Information), a classification based upon a strict need to know requirement and required during times and situations when our national security is not merely seriously threatened, but threatened gravely, such as being on the very verge of a nuclear war or actually engaged in one. As a qualified Nuclear Weapons

Employment Officer, I was grateful that the CIA's Gary Powers U-2 Soviet shootdown at the end of the Eisenhower administration, and the Cuban Missile Crisis at the beginning of that of Kennedy's were resolved peacefully. If they hadn't been I would have gotten that ultra Top Secret clearance and taken by an SSO (Special Security Officer) along with other Prefix 5 officers* to a SCIF (Sensitive Compartmental Intelligence Facility), shown satellite photographs, briefed on target locations and names or their coded designations, nuclear weapons availability and delivery means, weapons yield (kilotons or megatons), optimal heights of burst, radiological fallout patterns based on wind direction and speed, and perhaps bomb damage and casualty estimates. While in that sealed room of secret location deep underground somewhere I also would have available the latest ISUMS and PIRS (intelligence summaries and periodic intelligence reports).

In mid-August, 2022, FBI agents, with a search warrant issued by a local district magistrate, searched Trump's house at Mar-A-Lago in Palm Beach, Florida. They were so courteous I'm surprised the lead FBI man didn't bow to the person who answered the door. They recovered eleven sets of classified documents: three Coincidental, three Secret, and five Top Secret, to include one that contained Sensitive Compartmented Information. A trove of such incriminating evidence should leave the former President open to charges of violation of the Espionage Act, obstruction of justice, and

---

* Prefixes to MOS (Military Occupational Specialties [my basic branch was designated 1542-Infantry]) identified more definitive specialties; prefix 5 indicated Nuclear Weapons Employment Officer, as a prefix 7 would indicate parachutist.

the mishandling or even criminal handling of government documents, to include the destruction of such documents (recall those in the White House toilets). As to Trump's claim that he, as President, has the authority to declassify documents is utter nonsense; those to be declassified or destroyed are subject to strict rules in doing so, and by law, not even a President can declassify Top Secret SCI documents that deal with nuclear program matters.

Despite all this, newscasters and pundits still are speculating about Trump's running for President and when he might announce his intention of doing so. My view is that should he make such an announcement he should do it from his cell in the Federal Detention Barracks at Leavenworth, Kansas. Even as I write he should be facing charges and specifications brought by what those investigators found at Mar-A-Lago. But Trump is a very cunning cove. He knows that if he were to be arrested and charged as would any other malefactor in this country there is the fear of a real insurrection in America, one that would make that at the Capitol on January 6th, 2021, look like a Sunday School picnic. To that, I say let it come. As I've written elsewhere, there would be considerable bloodshed, but if the bulk of our armed forces remain loyal to the oaths they took, the insurrectionists could never win. But if Trump manages to hit the ball into the tall grass again, as he has during his many transgressions during the last five years, if he manages to do so in the most precarious strait he's been in, you should recall also what I've said about the current state of our judicial system, which is in such sad disarray. Think of true Justice. Finally, think also of what is contained in those classified documents; certain of which could serve as the death warrants of agents and sources, both domestic and foreign, in various parts of the world, should their contents be revealed.

I hope this dissertation will help to clarify the position in this mainly uniformed, confused conjecture on the part of newscasters and their "expert" contributors concerning Trump and his destruction of White House records and absconding to his perceived refuge at Mar-A-Lago, taking with him voluminous classified documents.* His trying to flush other documents down those antiquated White House toilets should provide *Saturday Night Live* and the other late night TV comics some useful material. I do wonder, increasingly, when the American public will come to realize that Trump now is merely another citizen, whatever he and his misguided followers may think otherwise. Yes, with certain prerequisites but with no official status. No one is above the law. Depending on what's in those documents found at Mar-A-Lago, Trump could be imprisoned for life; if we were at war he could be executed.† Well, enough of these little restful reflections; let us continue our ramble with a visit to Addicts Avenue.

---

* If I were back on active duty and mishandled a classified document, even one marked Confidential, I'd be facing a jail sentence now, not for the document's contents, but for mishandling a classified document. Of course, the contents are why the document was classified and I would have broken a Federal Law. Even documents marked "Secret" can be SCI (Sensitive Compartmented Information) or even higher, more sensitive classification.
† I wouldn't be surprised to learn he never even had a security clearance at all (waived by Executive Privilege somehow), as any private citizen with a history such as Trump's couldn't even get clearance for "confidential." It is inconceivable to me that Trump should be in any position to run for President in 2024.

17

Several years ago I saw and heard on cable or network news—it may have been a segment on the usually reliable CBS weekly program *60 Minutes*—that while the U.S. comprises less than five percent of the world's population, it consumes sixty-five percent of its illicit drugs. That's stale news with today's rapidly moving events, but if the numbers have changed they certainly haven't changed for the better. Now let me give you some other figures, from the archives of that Oracle of the Internet, Google. The death rate in 2019 from drug overdoses was 78,630, up four percent from the previous year. The death toll between 2019 and 2020 rose twenty-nine percent, to 100, 306. So now we can say that we have an epidemic within a pandemic; something akin to suffering two wounds simultaneously, when the pain from the more severe wound masks to some extent, and in some cases completely, that of the lesser. There were 108,000 deaths from drug overdoses during the first half of 2022. That's one every hour.

When several crises come in different forms, as in the threats we now are facing, they tend to mask one another. After all, how many can we countenance and endure and try to control and defend ourselves against at the same time? To name a few, there is the lack of any gun control among civilians and the resultant murder of thousands of innocent people, in great part children, that also has reached crisis proportions; the very real possibility of war with Russia over the fate of Ukraine, or with China over the future of

Taiwan, at a time when we are in a state of sociopolitical domestic divisiveness and in the worst possible condition to fight a cohesive, cooperative war,* either conventional or nuclear. Then there is the looming specter of climate change which increasingly refuses to be overshadowed by those more imminent crises. Floods, forest fires, tornadoes, hurricanes, typhoons (in the Pacific), and perhaps more important, heat waves and droughts that are becoming more frequent and more severe. The Greenland ice cap is melting steadily;† the oceans have already risen two feet, which means as only one example, that Miami will be under water in the not too distant future, and in many parts of the world people will begin to starve to death from the lack of agricultural products due to drought; and those of you who have managed to survive will be grateful for a drink of potable water. Added to the food shortages is the loss of the vital supply of grain shipped worldwide from the Ukrainian Port of Odesa on the Black Sea by the Russian blockade there.

I may have taken you beyond the precincts of Addicts Avenue a little, but I think it was for a worthwhile cause. Let us leave here with this bit of detail about the main culprits in this death by drugs. Other than the dealers and users, there are Methamphetamines and Fentanyl, the latter being exponentially more powerful than morphine, and with no antidote to save the victim(s) of either of them. While those two seem to be in a dead heat another

---

* As we did when we stood united and willing during World War II. In those days we had the We generation; today it's the Me variety.

† Already enough to fill 7.2 million Olympic-sized swimming pools or cover the entire State of West Virginia with a foot of water.

enchantress called Oxycontin or Oxycodone seems to be running a close second. The path to perdition may begin with the overprescribing of legitimate pain killers, then the self-condemned victim's resort to the "little white hag"* of heroin, and then to one of the fearsome killers named above. Recently, one hundred bags of Fentanyl were found with the dead body of a thirteen-year-old female suicide.

Since I see that Portly Place is no great distance away, let us pause there for a time. But first a little history about this neighborhood. Portly Place, once called simply "The Piggeries," since that was where hogs were bred, bought, and sold, was raised to a higher social level when the town council, having received so many complaints about its location, had its piggeries moved to a rural area. It then was thoroughly cleared and cleaned out. After the pig pens had been removed, along with the ramshackle sheds, sties and barns, new construction and landscaping was begun. Those unsightly and evil-smelling old structures were replaced with stately houses that were purchased by wealthy merchants, doctors, lawyers, and others of the town's "gentry," and others in the surrounding area. It then was renamed Portly Place. The name couldn't have been more apt, since as if to flaunt their relative affluence in those dreary days of the 1930s during the Great Depression, the residents of Portly

---

* Those of you who may be interested should read Francis Beeding's novel of the same name, published in the 1930s, that though fiction is very informative about heroin addiction; the same can be said of Eric Ambler's *A Coffin for Dimitrios*, published a few years later. Both books provide an excellent explication of how a tentative, even innocent interest in opiates, leading to a little experimentation can end in fully fledged and catastrophic addiction and often death. Ambler's book treats with all opiates.

Place, as if by mutual, collective concordance became so fat that they could be easily identified as residents of the newly transformed part of town. Before long there began to appear a number of those less fortunate people who attempted to imitate them (monkey see, monkey do), but unable to afford decent food, ate anything, thus gaining weight while at the same time ruining their health.

And thereby a tale can be told, or at least a little allegory to give some substance to Portly Place. The tale may do for the fat cats on Wall Street, and it was fun to write, but what about the rest of the obese people in this country, those mainly in the rural areas and the suburbs, which is not to say that they also have a substantial representation in urban areas? In urban settings, I'm sorry to say, it is the minority groups who seem to be beset with the problem of obesity more than the Caucasians.* This is not a racist statement; it merely is a fact based upon my own observations and fact-checking. In a broader, nationwide sense our problem with obesity, which may well become endemic, seems to be running rampant among those adamantine, unquestioning followers of former President Trump who have virtually sanctified him despite his mentally unbalanced fantasies and lies.† Look again at those videos and films that still are shown on network and cable TV newscasts of the 1/6 attack on the Capitol building and you will see them, man, woman, and boy. You will see them on TV commercials as well,

---

* That is not to say that the white people aren't doing their best to equal or even outweigh them.

† It was Plato who said that "the partisan, when he is engaged in a dispute, cares nothing about the right of the question, but is anxious only to convince his hearers of his own assertions."

thanks to the insidious plague of political correctness that insists on that other great lie of "I'm okay, you're okay"—the fat, the gaunt, tall, short, attractive, ugly, the intellectual, the half-witted—the list is practically endless. Political correctness dictates we must be all alike, equal in every way. In short, we must never do or say anything that may shake any individual's self-esteem. As I've said, you'll see the less fortunate, mainly physically, in TV commercials, except for filmed brief interviews with reporters, but you rarely will see them otherwise unless the part an actor is playing requires it; you will see our best and brightest and of course our more attractive actors. Has it become criminal or immoral for one to be grateful that by some accident of birth he doesn't look like Charles Laughton's portrayal of the hunchback of Notre Dame, or like Margaret Hamilton's witch in *The Wizard of Oz*? But there is one thing political correctness cannot do for fat people. I use the word "fat" purposefully because it is explicit and unclouded by euphemistic twaddle. Today we have "lame" for crippled, "impaired" for afflicted, "mentally impaired" for insane, and so on. But the exalted language of political correctness cannot make "overweight," or "heavy," or "full-figured," and yes, "portly" people less susceptible to diabetes, cardiovascular diseases, or, of prominent importance today, the COVID-19 virus and all its variants. Once again, I for one will not miss them, especially those who refused to be vaccinated for some specious reason, even if they succumbed to one or more of those potentially deadly ailments. This "I'm okay, you're okay" fantasy has also inspired those pathetic but much ballyhoo'd "Special

Olympics" that have become a kind of exhaltation of almost the entire spectrum of disabilities.*

There is another related matter to address before we leave this porcine neighborhood and that concerns the increasing obesity among so many of our law enforcement officers, at all levels. The "rookie" officers, when they first show up for duty are mostly pretty fit, especially if they engaged in sports when in their civilian schools and after they had gone through the physical training required in the police course they had just completed. But in too many cases that fitness doesn't endure, in good part owning to the examples set by their older brother officers.

Occasionally you might have an opportunity of observing a formation of police somewhere at some ceremonial event, perhaps to honor one of their fallen comrades or at the decoration ceremony of one of their more fortunate ones. See them standing in ranks, more or less at the position of attention, and looking more like the Pizza Eating & Beer Drinking Society of America than a contingent of keen-eyed guardians of law and order.

---

* Look up "basket case" in a dictionary published in 1976 or earlier and you'll find: "one who has had all four limbs amputated." The term was used to describe soldiers who had been totally dismembered in the Great War and were literally kept in baskets in remote wards of VA hospitals. The name was coined in 1919 and was in common use until it was obliterated, since no other term could diminish its harsh reality. If such horrors are to be kept from us how then in this age of "I'm okay, you're okay" the Shriner's Children's Hospital in their TV begging show us a small child whose one hand grows completely out of his shoulder while the other grows out of eight inches of his "arm" and tells us "I can walk!" as the camera reveals the metal braces he wears on both his deformed legs.

With all the dashboard and body cameras and closed circuit TV cameras everywhere today you'll see police officers much more often on network or cable news outlets when they are "in action." So here they come, many with uniforms stretched to near bursting point, pistols raised, perhaps one or two of them armed with that small caliber (.223 or 5.6 mm) but lethal hypervelocity AR-15 (such as the one that "accidentally" killed an innocent girl in the dressing room of a Los Angeles store not long ago). And then, once they have arrived "on the scene," there is their language. Some men who find themselves in a tense, even a dangerous situation, and fear only for their own lives and safety, have a tendency, more a compulsion actually, to punctuate their speech with obscene interjections; it's effing this and effing that, whomever they may be shouting at. They seem unable to speak calmly, whether they must speak loudly to be heard and understood, or in a situation when speaking calmly and relatively quietly would be more conducive to resolving the confrontation. With few exceptions the law enforcement officers I have described are physical cowards who think somehow that foul, boisterous language will mask their fear. Soldiers and policemen have a kinship in this regard, although soldiers with their adversaries are usually pretty evenly matched in close combat. It is this cowardice combined with a lack of compassion, compunction, and conscience that leads to incidents such as a law officer emptying a fourteen-round magazine into the back of an unarmed, suspected malefactor who is running away in fear for his own precious life. Infinitely worse, in Akron, Ohio, in late May 2022, was the shooting of Jayland

Walker, a young, unarmed black man after a routine traffic stop, forty-six times by eight policemen. Add to this the astonishing fact that as the target *de jour*, twenty-five-year-old Walker was *handcuffed behind his back* when his body arrived at the medical examiner's office. News reports tell us that it will take several months for any decision to make any prosecution(s).*

There is another reason for such scurvy acts as that which I have just described, and that reason should be obvious by the main topic I am addressing: that of obesity. A fat police officer almost certainly is in no condition to jog very far, to say nothing of running the length of a football field. A twelve-year-old child could outdistance him. But we are in the day of bullets before brawn; bullets and brawn on TV and movie screens are reserved for protagonists who usually are on the right side of the law. The "suspect," if indeed he or she is suspected of anything, cannot outrun a bullet, let alone fourteen of them, to say nothing of forty-six of them. Even if that "guardian of peace" were able to overtake his quarry, in too many cases he might not be able to subdue him and take him into custody, so it's a case of being Tasered or shot dead.

The capable actor William Conrad appeared in a TV series entitled *Cannon* for a time. Conrad was, as House

---

* As I've said elsewhere, the longest course of training to qualify for police duty in the U.S. is twenty weeks; in Germany, as only one example, it is three years for duty at all levels. Vainglorious police chiefs at municipal levels are seen wearing four or even five (circled) stars, once reserved for the very highest officers in our Armed Forces, on their collars or epaulettes bring to my mind little girls playing "dress-up in their mommies' shoes and clothing."

Speaker Nancy Pelosi once described Donald Trump, morbidly obese. Though he played the part of a private investigator who once had been an official policeman, the description was apt. His physical appearance could have changed little since in the days of radio when he spoke the part of *The Lone Ranger*. No longer able to hide on radio, when the program appeared on TV he was replaced by Clayton Moore, whose physique was suitable for spurring on his horse with a hearty "Hiyo, Silver, away!" rather than having to coax him to move under such a ponderous burden. Along with his faithful Indian sidekick, Tonto (meaning "stupid" in Spanish), played on TV by Jay Silver Heels, Conrad could have provided us with some great low comedy.

I recall now that as a boy growing up on one of those barrier islands off the south New Jersey coast, those State Police Officers, organized, trained, and even uniformed by Colonel Schwarzkopf, father of "Stormin' Norman" Schwarzkopf, the General who commanded the Desert Storm invasion of Iraq in 1993. They all looked to me like tall, lean, clean-shaven giants. I discovered when I was older that they were required to be at least five feet eleven inches tall and of a weight not to exceed the rigid height-weight chart established by the Colonel, who also had designed their uniforms. Two of them would come to my four-room, red brick schoolhouse and talk to us periodically about civic responsibilities and safe practices at home and elsewhere; crossing streets safely, and so on. They were (to me) resplendent in their teal-blue tunics, gold-striped black breeches, and gleaming black knee boots. To compare them to so many of the policemen and women I see today seems a sacrilege.

Many years ago, in the early 1950s, the 11th Airborne Division was stationed at Fort Campbell, Kentucky and commanded by a general whose name I won't reveal, since even though I'm certain he has gone to that Great Bivouac in the Sky, there's always his progeny to consider. I see no harm, however, in giving you a couple of sobriquets by which he was known in the ranks, among the soldiers themselves of course. The general, at least in physical appearance, was not what might be called the poster boy of the American paratrooper, and was known familiarly as "Pear Shape," or "Shaped Charge." These aphorisms came not from disrespect but from physical fact. He was decidedly overweight, especially in the lower parts of his body, and his shoulder width did not do anything to compensate for this. The General went on extended leave, and it was rumored that he had a "medical condition" that had to be resolved. The Assistant Commanding Officer carried on in his absence. When "Pear Shape" returned he had changed remarkably, at least in appearance. He looked fit and trim, and it was immediately apparent that he had lost a considerable amount of weight.

Now in those days, as I'm sure it is today with an adjustment for inflation, paratroopers received what is called hazardous duty pay, that had recently been raised from $100 per month to $110 for officers and for enlisted personnel, half that. Situated where it is, Fort Campbell was no great distance from Nashville, Tennessee where the Grand Ol' Opry held forth on weekends. After Saturday morning inspections a goodly number of enlisted men and some officers drove down Highway 41A to join in the festivities, and of course this required a car, so that extra $55 a month fit the payments on a new car nicely (in those days). Of course the General knew this as well as anyone, and not long after his return a directive came down to all units regarding "Weight Standards for Parachutists." I should have mentioned that hazardous duty pay included the proviso that those drawing it had to make at least one jump every three months. In itself this was a sensible requirement for maintaining proficiency and presented no problem, with the usual training exercises, getting a jump with another unit, and so on. But now, due to the newly reshaped Commanding General and his newly directed height-weight requirements, there were those, including Mess and Supply Sergeants, Company Clerks, Chaplain's Assistants, even First Sergeants, and somewhat ironically, the General's own driver, who were seen walking around with a troubled look. "Hit 'em in the pocketbook!" the General was heard to tell members of his staff. Even the G-4 (Logistics) seemed to be somewhat concerned when seen at the Officer's Club. But the General's campaign, though somewhat harsh and to some a little underhanded, was a success. There was a visible rise in morale, what soldiers call *esprit de corps*, and one could sense it when one of the Regimental Combat Teams went on parade. Would that we could do the same, barring the jumping out of perfectly good airplanes, with our porky policemen and women.

And just incidentally, as I write restaurant associations throughout the country are clamoring for that twenty-eight billion-dollar aid package that Congress is considering to "help restaurants to survive." Why not instead put it in a fund for children who wouldn't have lunch if they didn't get it free at school?

Since we're still here in Portly Place, let's linger a little longer while we make a visit to the local Police Station; the relatively more affluent residents insisted they have law enforcement in the vicinity.

So here we are, in this haven of order and discipline. Ah yes, there we see the ubiquitous British horsehair dartboard, hung on a wall at about the proper height but never used, as we've seen it in so many police procedurals on TV. There are other familiar objects in the room: Styrofoam cups full of cold coffee, other taller drink receptacles of various kinds that had contained some kind of soft drink, including those called "slurpies," half-empty pizza and doughnut boxes, and here and there one that may have held a Danish pastry or a croissant for the more discriminating diner. There was a time when, in an office dealing with such serious matters, one would see only a water cooler, and perhaps in a corner, a small table with the makings for instant coffee. In bygone days being found with food and drink on your desk for a second time could be cause for dismissal. Just because you didn't take your lunch break in the cafeteria or in that little restaurant around the corner didn't mean you were getting any more work done than was expected of you, unless of course everyone was working through an emergency. And oh yes, I failed to mention that in this same room we found that there were cellophane bags (or whatever they're using now to add to that plastic mess the size of France in the

Pacific Ocean) of deep-fried Fritos, Tostitos, Cheetos, and Doritos; even those good old potato chips, some full, others not, everywhere; the kind of "food" that turns you into what the Germans call *Schmalz* (a tub of grease).*

And with that I think we should leave and move on to Racial Road, while the TV commercials promote their deathburgers and other schmaltzy delectables and Americans continue to eat and drink everywhere: on the street, in their cars, on public transportation, at their places of work, in theatres, and even in the halls of Congress. And in college football† we now have the Cheese-it and Chick Fil A Peach Bowls to add to the Sugar Bowl. And so on to Racial Road.

---

* The Germans coined the phrase "your teeth will dig your grave," and they weren't talking about dental hygiene (except in special cases).

† College football now has become the minor leagues of the National Football League.

18

Elsewhere I have written at some length about racism, focusing on the salient question: Will racism ever disappear? and I concluded that the short answer was, no. But after giving that blunt answer more consideration I decided that if there were a change it would be conditional, and something as trivial as a child's toy helped bear this out. The toy was a child's doll. This little doll was not in the image of a little white girl or boy that since time immemorial has been the accepted standard for dolls,* at least in the Western world, nor was it in the more reasonable image of a black child and just another sop for the antiracialists. No; it was in the image of a biracial child, and that was what supported my final conclusion on the matter. Briefly, what I have decided is that racism, like those glaciers in Greenland, will fall under its own weight, *sua sponte* (of its own accord), however you may wish to say it, at least in the way it manifests itself today, when all mankind has become to some extent anatomically similar, with all the biracial contact today and in the foreseeable future (assuming mankind has a future). When skin color has universally

---

* Why did Walt Disney entitle that amiable, engaging, animated little movie of the late 1930s *Snow White and the Seven Dwarfs*? He did it because he never imagined that he couldn't or shouldn't do it; that title was accepted without engendering any controversy. Can you imagine the audience reception of a film called *Coal Black and the Seven Sambos* in those *Gone With the Wind* days? They well might think it was just a little low comedy and expect to see pork chops growing on trees and watermelons everywhere, as in a movie I saw years ago about a Black's concept of Heaven.

133

become the shade of *cafe latte*. I used that conditional "at least" above because though uniformity of skin color would reduce the more blatant aspects of racism significantly (the pot calling the kettle black), it would not eliminate racism completely.

Of course, an anthropologist in consultation with an anatomist would tell you that other physical changes, a blending of physiognomy, might take a thousand years or more. So my final conclusion must be that although there may be a universal similarity in skin color several generations from now, a universal and complete physical affinity can only be contemplated in the misty future, if ever. So it would seem that I was right and still wrong in my final conclusion. In any case, anyone who reads this will no longer be around to verify or abnegate my predictions, nor will the antiracists and the political correctness advocates find them of much or any use to them today.*

Nonetheless, despite all the pressures of political correctness and our civil rights laws we never will be able to end racism by trying to legislate it away any more than we could atheism or telling people what kind of music they should listen to. And unlike the contagious diseases the white colonists introduced to unsuspecting hundreds of thousands of native inhabitants throughout the world there are no vaccines to neutralize racism.

---

* Miscegenation, the marriage or cohabitation of persons of different races, was prohibited by the laws of fifteen southern and border States until 1967 when the Supreme Court declared those laws to be unconstitutional because they violated the equal protection clause of the Fourteenth Amendment. Somewhat ironically, the restrictions on State powers were designed primarily to protect freed negroes.

Truly, "people of color" have been, still are, and will be for the foreseeable future, victims of prejudice and discrimination, the latter word once a perfectly innocent one but that now has suffered the same fate as "gay" thanks to that self-appointed guardian of "righteousness" we call political correctness. That "people of color" I have chosen to describe these victims is simply another euphemism that succeeded "colored people." Then came "Blacks," which has faded into obscurity if only because of its impreciseness; "Afros" or "African Americans" and "Afro Americans" were tried but now seem to have failed simply for their preciseness. "Black is Beautiful" never had much if any success, probably because it was considered inept or inappropriate by so many people who were steeped in Caucasian standards of beauty, and, dare I say it? even by a number of Blacks who wished they were white.* Now we are witnessing a veritable tidal wave of "Black Lives Matter," on banners, posters, placards, and even legible clothing and the like.

As long as we (and they) keep trying to find an inoffensive name or a term of reference for African Americans, which is what they are, and for those others of mixed races, Biracial Americans, or even Eurafricans, as in Eurasians, racism will persist. It seems clear to me that until we come up with something acceptable to almost everyone, we'll be in

---

* At the Oracle of Google you will find the lyrics to a song that acquired dubious popularity in the 1930s, played and sung by "Fats" Waller and Louis "Satchmo" Armstrong. The song is entitled "Black and Blue," which sums up the lyrics. On his return from a world tour, Armstrong alleged that the song was a big hit with his African audiences. This was about the time when Toni Morrison, the successful novelist, was praying that she could have blue eyes.

a quandary about this. Little or nothing can be done to eradicate racism until in some remote or existent future we humans, as a species of animals, all look more or less alike in physical appearance. Until then, if there is to be a then, African Americans, despite certain cosmetic attempts, to include what we, and they, choose to call them, will be "different," different than the Western (European or colonial, which gave it impetus) "norm" of Caucasians. And at the root of this deep-seated tendency is the xenophobia which has permeated this nation since its inception. In the estimation of a very great number of Caucasian Americans, Asians, Hispanics, and especially Africans, are "different," if nothing more objectionable, and I include those white people who, in many cases because of politically correct reasons, won't admit it. I haven't mentioned native Americans, from whom we literally stole this land, since they, as a race, hardly seem to exist any longer, so little is ever said about them.

I never had any interest in dolls, unless you'd care to broaden the definition a bit, but did have in the late 1950s and in those eventful 1960s several young daughters who did. Those were the days of Easy Bake Ovens,* the Barbie doll, and later dolls, because the manufacturers were seeking a bigger market for the prototypical Caucasian image of the blue-eyed, blond, pert little original. Now there appeared Barbie(s) across the spectrum of post-puberty; slim and lithe little beauties that conformed to accepted (white) standards.

---

* In the days when "proper" mommies stayed home, took care of their children, and baked cookies. The child's Easy Bake Oven was a miniature version of her oven often given to little girls at Christmastime or on their birthdays. Their little brothers got Red Ryder lever-action B-B guns, unless they preferred to play with their sister's dolls.

A little later there appeared a male doll named "Ken," Barbie's boyfriend. Many somewhat different Barbies, but just one Ken, who must have been a very busy young man.

But I must delay for a moment in giving you my view of the root cause(s) of this victimization. As you read what follows, whatever your own beliefs, you can rest assured that I believe, one could say with metaphysical certitude, that in this continuing controversy no truer or more just statement has been or could be made than the assertion I cited above: Black lives matter. What greater gift can humans be grateful for than life itself, despite all the ills, great and small, we must endure while we are living it? We have been endowed, somehow, with an intellect and a free will, and have abused both to our own cost, not merely in this matter of racism. We could do better, in a host of ways.*

Yes, Blacks (I'll use that word now, imprecise as it may be) have been victimized, especially in this country. Some would call it simply fate; others would ascribe it to the even more nebulous "God's will," as in "The Mark of Ham," and still others would refer to Blacks as "children of a lesser god." Putting all theological or philosophical causes aside, I call it simply a vagary of evolution; and now I must ask your indulgence for my having to use some mind-jarring terms. I see it as an anthropological, anthropometrical eventuality on the erratic evolutionary path a fickle Mother Nature chose for us to become what we are today, all of us, with various physical and characteristic qualities, the most readily

---

* To cite merely one dismal example, in a little more than the last 3000 years of recorded history there have been little more than 200 years of relative peace.

identifiable of them, color. The rest of the victimization's *raison d'etra* is purely sociocultural throughout the known history of mankind. (Now give me a moment to catch my breath while you reach for a dictionary.)

I think it only fair, since I've noted a few euphemistic labels for these victims, to give you some that are less flattering. Prepare yourselves. For the Blacks we have (or had): nigger,* coon, jig or jigaboo, spook, shine, dinge, ironhead, shade or shade 51,† night fighter (military), darky, jungle bunny, monkey, moolanjon (from the Italian *melanzane*, eggplant, i.e., black), pickaninny (a black child). For Asians—we no longer use the word Oriental but we've retained Occidental (Western, European)—we have, dink, slope, slant-eye, flat face, gook, chink, Jap, Flip (Filipino), and WOG, from the British colonialists' failed attempt to ban racial slurs; "Worthy Oriental Gentleman" quickly became just WOG. For the Latinos or Hispanics, as they call themselves, there are greasers, mestizos,‡ or wetbacks (as they emerged on our side of the Rio Grande). And

---

* I find this condemnation and *de facto* exclusion from our vocabulary unjust, since its derivation from the Latin *nigro*, simply means the color black. Then, in the semi-literate South, it became nigra, and then to the nationwide nigger. The words niggard and niggardly (meaning stingy) somehow are still holding their own in our lexicons. The Commissioner of the Fire Department of New York City, Daniel Nigro (an Italian American) now pronounces his name Nygro, as in hydro. This is more than unfair; it's ungrammatical; for more than 2000 years nigro has been pronounced neegro.

† In the Army's catalogue of colors, black is designated as "shade 51." I once served in a regiment in which a black company commander was jokingly and openly referred to as "Captain Midnight" (of TV notability at the time) by his fellow officers; and more discretely within the other ranks.

‡ Indian-European ancestry.

for our Islamic enemies or "friends," dirt bags, ragheads, sand niggers, or Gyppos (Egyptians). As for the "injuns" or "redskins" whose homeland we expropriated, we now merely ignore them. All this transcends the xenophobia that permeates much of our country; it is closer to a state of vitriolic dehumanization, and anyone known by such derogatory and viciously biting labels is a victim of our entire system of socialization worldwide.*

We never will fully understand this matter of racism without an examination of "Western" sociocultural history. An indelible criterion for our preferences in human anatomical beauty has been emplaced upon mankind dating back several thousand years. The statuary found in parthenons and pantheons of the ancient Greeks or Romans exemplify this. Say what you will about Soloman's lust for the Queen of Sheebah, she cannot be included in the assemblage of Greco-Roman art I have alluded to. And after all, Cleopatra†

---

* As a mere advisory, I should note that in their zealous efforts to fight racism, progressive Democrats are in good part responsible for the increasing number of "people of color" on TV, especially on the network or cable news outlets, and not least in so many commercials, with sponsors being advised that their products may be boycotted if this isn't done (the days of "quota" or "token" persons of color are over, and Afros now have been given important roles). However well-meant this effort may be, it might well produce a backlash among white separatists by stirring up more of their annoyance and hostility. In a more subtle way, it may even serve to bring them some converts to their cause; people who have remained mainly noncommittal on their feelings about racism but who have had enough of the progressive Democrats' propaganda. TV in America has become a café of all nations, and more is not always better.

† My old philosophical friend and namesake Blaise Pascal wrote almost four hundred years ago: "Cleopatra, had her nose been shorter, the whole face of the world would have been changed."

was the daughter of a Greek. So for the purpose of this exposition let us set aside skin color, which I think has been discussed adequately anyway, and consider other physical characteristics without, I hope, giving undue offense.

For those of you who may be unacquainted with the ancient statuary that I have alluded to, most Americans are aware of such modern day beauties as Ava Gardner, Rhonda Fleming, Elizabeth Taylor, and any number of today's models such as Christie Brinkley and Cindy Crawford. Even the TV news outlets have such "European" beauties as Kirsten Powers and Melanie Zanona. All these latter-day, living examples could have been candidates for inclusion in those temples and pantheons of two or three thousand years ago. Incidentally, to be fair in the choice of the images of men, to whom the same or at least equal standards of preferences apply, I was remiss in not citing Michaelangelo's statue of Apollo, to say nothing of that of David, both the quintessential models of physical manhood. So it is this that gives the lie to and makes hollow such expressions as "Black is Beautiful," and gives substance to that other, "Beauty is in the eye of the beholder." The interpretation of beauty varies in concept with different societies. Many of those we call racists have a preset, indelible, mind-set. Unjust? yes, even unfair, but a reality we all must face. Would there have been so much publicity in the news media of the West in the case of pretty, blond Madelein McCann, who was kidnapped in Portugal and presumably killed fifteen years ago if she had been the child of African parents?*

---

* Western culture, especially in the matter of physical appearance, is so ingrained in so many of us that true racial integration won't occur for the foreseeable future, if ever. It has taken 60 million years to reach our present state of multi-racial physical appearance as humans.

The victims, or objects if you choose, of these preferences are fully aware of what they are faced with. Despite the seeming injustice, they have had to accept their fate, and their only means of coping with it is to emulate, if not imitate, those whom fate has somehow favored. Ava Gardner, one of my exemplars in the continuum of preferential beauty, played the rôle of "Julie" in a film version of Jerome Kern's *Showboat.** Julie had an indiscernible trace of negro blood and so was able to "pass" (as a white woman) in those days of Jim Crow.† She was careful with her speech patterns, and diction; she even had a white husband. In the South in those days such an impersonation as hers was a criminal offense, so her husband was willing to mix his blood with hers, literally, and so face imprisonment along with her. Ultimately, they had to pack up and leave their jobs on the showboat and find a more tolerant place in which to live.

But what can the great majority of blacks, and others, do? Aside from skin color what other physical characteristics do the racists find objectionable and even repugnant in their concept of beauty. Feeling somewhat apologetic, I will delineate them: bulbous noses and flaring nostrils, hypertrophied lips, gapped upper front teeth, hyper-recessive hairlines and hair that is the antithesis of what those with a predilection for "Western" standards of beauty would

---

* Which opens with "Ol' Man River" and Oscar Hammerstein's lyrics, "Here we all live on the Mississippi, here we all work while the white man play…" echoing Fritz Lang's "The rich play above while the poor toil below" in his film *Metropolis*.

† Other quaint designations for "colored people" were, high yellow (yeller, yaller), octoroon or quadroon (descendent of a negro great-grandparent or grandparent). Lena Horne and Harry Belafonte, singers and actors, are examples of both genders.

refer to as "a woman's crowning glory"—plentiful silken luxuriant natural blond or auburn hair—which requires them to wear a hat in certain Christian churches. Black, wiry hair arranged in bizarre configurations, or a hairline that leaves a woman half-bald might provide a different reason for covering their heads. Lower in the body our devotee of occidental beauty is not pleased to see massive breasts, elephantine thighs, or a hypertrophied *glutei maximi* (prominent buttocks).*

The contemporary compensatory measures taken by so many Blacks to mitigate this disparity in acceptable appearance can only be described as grotesque, by any standards. At the same time many Blacks, of both genders, have chosen to alleviate if not solve this dilemma by shaving themselves bald, and some take a second step and wear wigs, often blond, which in many cases makes them look as silly as white people wearing black-face in a minstrel show. A current example of this is the "blond" "high yellow" girl on TV in the Audi commercial. Meanwhile, as I write, eighteen HBCU (Historic Black Colleges and Universities) have received bomb threats. I should think that Blacks have had enough problems without that.

We have reached a point in the history of this planet when the omnipresent and seemingly overwhelming and increasingly inevitable threat of global climate change could presage the end of all life as we know it. If there is to be any hope for our survival, it is time when we as the

---

* Still, if an alien visiting Earth saw our Miss Universe, it might throw up its claws and slither back to its space ship screaming. Again, beauty is in the eye of the beholder.

only "intelligent" species of life on Earth have any chance of avoiding the Apocalypse. We may still be able to save ourselves for a time, but to have any chance of doing so we must face the threat of extinction as a cohesive cooperative force, regardless of race.

Racism and prejudice and envy, yes envy, with all its frustration and rage exists on the part of those races who see themselves as the victims of a great anthropological injustice. I am sorry to conclude that if we must face that Apocalypse we will find that there is a fifth horseman named Racial Injustice. As for me, I don't pity those victims—pity is such a final and useless emotion—but I do sympathize with them and do understand what they must feel about their (as yet) unavailing desire for "equality."* And I do praise the great majority of Asians in this country who have not felt driven to alter their eyes surgically. As we leave this long and doleful Racial Road I want to say that in my predicting of grave events and giving you an occasional date as we ramble along, some of you may think what I have been presenting for your consideration is an amateurish imitation of the predictions

---

* Still photos of the late George Floyd and W. Kamau Bell, an antiracial activist and producer of the TV documentary "United Shades of America," show them posed with a pseudo intellectual forefinger touching a full or pendulous lip and a thoughtful expression, much as are representations of certain European men who were or are notable. Of interest also is that black celebrities not infrequently marry Caucasians or the "high yellow" females. I can cite: Sammy Davis to actress Mae Britt, Tiger Woods to a blond, blue-eyed beauty; Herschel Walker and the late Kobe Bryant to "black" women with Caucasian physiognomies. I don't consider Supreme Court Justice Thomas a celebrity nor his white wife a beauty. Whatever the current state of racism is in this country, there is just enough smoke for there to be a fire smoldering under the surface of our societal fabric.

of Nostradamus combined with the diaries of Sam. Pepys. I freely admit that not having the prescience of the former nor the ability of the latter, I would never attempt such a challenging task.

What did I think of that town we just rambled through, named Prototypical, U.S.A. by the way? Well, what was it they used to say about New York City before the place became full of strangers? "It's okay for a visit, but I wouldn't like to live there." I'd say Prototypical isn't even a nice place to visit, let alone to live in.

Albert Einstein, in his probing the mysteries of time and space, once said that if it weren't for time, with its progressive movement forward and consequent changes, everything would be happening at once. As difficult as such a condition is to imagine, I find myself picturing Julius Caesar dancing with Marie Antoinette at my senior prom. I suggest you don't try to imagine such a state of affairs or you might think you're losing your mind; it's something like trying to grasp the actual meaning of infinity, or eternity, which is beyond our intellectual ability or capacity, as it was Einstein's, or Hawking's', or before them Newton's, or in even more distant times da Vinci's, or Galileo's, and back to the ancient Greeks. Today it is the causation of the so-called "Big Bang" and the almost pathetic presumption that our latest device to probe into the mysteries of the universe, the Webb telescope (assuming it works properly) will give us the "answers" to these insoluble, unfathomable mysteries.

19

So after that little metaphysical interjection let us go on about time, if only as we know and understand it. It was Ben Franklin who said "Time is money," and in a country such as ours, where the love of wealth is the veritable axis on which our world turns, it is not to be wasted. I find it difficult, almost impossible to understand that given that observation is correct, we, and especially our government, at all levels, waste so much time, and money, fruitlessly. Of course, if global climate change, like Nemesis seeking her revenge for our self-inflicted, indifferent exploitation of the only reasonably safe haven we almost certainly ever will have in this inexplicably vast universe dooms us, time will become a matter of little or no consequence. The final act will be an end of time, at least for those of us who may still exist when the final curtain comes down.

Aside from pride, avarice, and the rest of those deadly sins, with avarice leading the rest, the obsession with the acquisition and maintenance of wealth will have played its part. You can add to that the fact that most of the people who could have helped to save us all, globally, not merely by their lusting for power and wealth, have been of an age where they could be indifferent to the inevitable and final result; in brief, they knew and continue to know that they in all likelihood won't be here to see and suffer it. If there is any "saving grace" in this doomsday scenario at all it lies in the very nature of humankind itself, and in that very fragile and tenuous characteristic of hope. "Hope springs eternal" we say. Would that we could grasp the true meaning of that word "eternal," and if that were the case we should make the most of it, and time would still be of some importance.

There are many optimists whose spirits are almost impossible to dampen, for a variety of reasons: psychological, physiological, and even psychosomatic traits that are always flattering. These people see the glass as always half-full, never half-empty; who cleave, much like the fabled Pollyanna, to that Latin tag *carpe diem* (seize the day, it's later than you think), or to Robert Herrick's poetical exhortation to maidens to give up their virginity: "Gather thee rosebuds while ye may / Old Time is still a flying, / and this same flower that smiles today / tomorrow will be dying." All well and good, in its way. But for more verification of this sometimes seemingly senseless optimism look around you, or if you happen to be quarantined due to the pandemic, watch the news on TV. You won't see or hear any advisories about not burying your head in the sand because you'll drown when the tide comes in; oh no, but if you listen to and watch the hard news (and interpret it) you may think that nothing of any consequence has changed in our lives to any great extent. The commercials, with one or two exceptions, and the "entertainment" programs are essentially unchanged, and with almost religious fervor sports events, much like those spiritual requirements and observations that many religions require in order to ensure salvation, have been crowded into their usual channels on TV in order to make their seasons complete. As always this is driven by the drive for profit, for the teams and not least for the sponsors and TV stations, such as NBC when they charged sponsors seven million dollars for thirty-second commercials during the last Super Bowl game. All this is to the detriment of honest efforts to control the viral pandemic, and more proof that the acquisition of wealth is at the bottom of virtually everything today and as it has been since the founding of this Republic. There is little more I can say or suggest about this obsession with money, in or out of this country, except to curse the ancient Persians who introduced the use of money rather than staying with the practice of barter, or the Jews who invented banks and usury.* So given the futility of trying to tame that obsession with the acquisition of wealth what can we do in the time left to us, whether it be short or, by some miraculous intervention, long enough not to be a matter of concern to those of us who see life, with all its pain and problems, as a great gift for we mere mortals?

Given the dire straits in which we find ourselves, to a great extent of our own making, and the vicissitudes of human nature, what should we do? More to the point, what can we do while we still have time, however tentatively? It took more than nine years for the courts to settle the suit brought by the families of the twenty small children and six adults who were murdered at the Sandy Hook School in Connecticut on December 14th 2012.† Finally, a court ruling

---

* The Persians used bits of stone or bronze of various denominations as money. In Venice during the Middle Ages the Jews, unbridled by the Christian laws forbidding usury, set out their tables and benches (*bancos*, whence came the name banks) outside their houses and loaned money there, gaining profit from interest charged, a practice Christians were forbidden to engage in under penalty of death.
† In addition to the infamous behavior of the responders at Uvalde, Texas, the murders of those children at Columbine, Sandy Hook, and Parkland will always be etched in my memory.

found against the Remington Arms company who spawned the Bushmaster model of Colt's AR-15, the weapon that did the mass killing. The families were awarded $73,000,000 in total, but no amount of money can compensate a parent for such a shocking loss of a child, any child, but especially when that child is only five or six years old, and was killed so brutally, with all of his or her life to live.* This speaks almost precisely for the more recent tragedy at Uvalde, Texas. Still, that court's finding put a crack in the NRA's wall, and in that of their toadies in Congress.

We squander time; waste it in pursuits that are not of first importance to our future. A prime example of this is found in the sluggish proceedings of that bilateral committee that is investigating the 1/6 fracas at the Capitol that has announced that it will reveal its findings in full in the Fall of 2022. The salient question of crucial consequence here is, *when* in the Fall of 2022? If it is before the Congressional midterm elections and has damaging, even disastrous results for Trump and his henchmen, all well and good for the sake of justice and our future. But should such revelations be made after those elections, it appears increasingly probable that the Republicans and their *de facto* leader, Trump, will take control of the Congress, and that should he run again, and despite his present jeopardy over those classified documents,

---

* The civil suit(s) against that criminal commentator Alex Jones, who denied the mass killing ever even occurred, goes on in favor of the plaintiff(s). But what price can serve true justice to compensate for the killing of a child and subsequent pain inflicted by such a calloused act on the grief stricken parents? The Old Testament would require "an eye for an eye." Jones should be shot to death (with an AR-15), per *Lex Talionis*, the law of retribution or retaliation.

he may well regain the Presidency in 2024. Once again, time plays a key role, and actually a dual one since it was another waste of time that created this situation to begin with. If the lapse of time between the Presidential election on the 4th of November, 2020 and Biden's Inauguration on January 20, 2021, hadn't left Trump in the White House, with his Presidential powers still mainly intact, for more than two and one half months there almost certainly would have been no attack on the Capitol and no need for a cumbersome and costly investigation.* Once again, do you think we need some very important changes to our Constitution?

Time works both ways, depending on the situation, and perhaps the better word should be timing. When Putin decided to invade Ukraine he knew that the United States, informally, was the leader of NATO; he knew also that the U.S. was domestically in a state of turmoil, so he went in, to his cost as it seems to be turning out, mainly because he couldn't foresee the Ukrainians' stoic determination to resist or the European Union's cohesive effort to support and assist them. His timing was right but his intelligence organization failed him. In a totally different setting, politically, geographically, and historically, the Israeli's precipitated their Six-Day War with their Arab "enemies" with impeccable timing, just when we were recovering from the communist Tet Offensive in Vietnam and the Soviets were sending their tanks and troops into Prague to put down the uprising in Czechoslovakia.

---

* The Electoral College played a critical rôle, and provided more certain proof that it should be abolished.

Then there is the human factor to consider. The passage of time has a desensitizing, a deadening effect, on events and matters that may have shocked and even outraged right-thinking people throughout our nation at the time of their occurrence, but with the passage of time fade away and with more time even subside to a state of quiet indifference. One never hears the cry "Remember Pearl Harbor!" anymore, to say nothing of "Remember the Maine!" from the even dimmer past. You might find one or both of those two on a tatted sampler in the parlor of a nonagenarian couple in New England, and you'd have to ask a historian what the *Maine* was. As to "Remember the Alamo!" you can rely on Hollywood to remind you of that blot in our history books. In Ukraine, however patriotic her populous, "Remember Mariupol!" probably will similarly fade away.

But a better example is that relatively recent attack on those World Trade Towers, a tragedy that precipitated an unjustified war with Iraq and our profitless occupation of Afghanistan for twenty years, and ending in our blundering and humiliating departure. Even that last "outrage" has already begun to fade into the mists of time. More than a year has passed already since that portentous day of mayhem on Capitol Hill. Why was an investigation not begun immediately? One cannot help but recall the aftermath of the JFK assassination with its Warren Commission and other investigations and the controversies surrounding them; and still there exist lingering doubts about the "official" conclusions that were reached. Again, time settled the matter, at least to the insouciant satisfaction of the bulk of the populace, or perhaps I should have said the indifference that thrives with the passage of time.

Having mentioned the coming elections there are two other matters of essential importance worthy of our consideration, both of equal importance: one is passage of a just voting rights act, and the other enacting a Federal law denying States the right to redistricting, which violates the principles of homogeneity of popular interests, and equality of population in order to secure the future advantage of the party or group in control of a State legislature; and a concomitant advantage in Federal elections. At the top of Trump's stratagems is to ensure that neither of these restrictions is passed into law. As an adjunct to invoking those quintessential electoral safeguards in all future elections, both State and Federal, we should eliminate the filibuster. Once again, time will become a crucial factor in having accomplished these objectives in the running battle to preserve what is left of our democracy. I trust you can see that Time can be an invaluable ally, or it can be a deadly enemy, depending upon how one manages it. If Time is hostile, our best intentions can become victims of the indifferent and inexorable procession of events.

20

Has the time come, consistent with a Constitutional Convention, for a drastic change in our system of democratic governance? Could we make that change using a little of that benevolent, or enlightened despotism I spoke of earlier? From this point onward let us recall the words of Blaise Pascal, spoken centuries ago: "Justice without strength (power) is helpless; strength without justice is tyrannical"; and he ended this potent aphorism with: "Unable to make what is just strong, we have made what is strong just." That last dictum would certainly be true if Donald Trump were in charge of our ship of state, so we must make it our duty to keep him out of the wheelhouse.* In short, we must make what is just strong. Think of the protests we must endure over the mandates required to mitigate the ravages of this seemingly endless pandemic. Combined with the crises of uncontrolled shootings, homicide run rampant actually, and the ever increasing epidemic of drug addiction and its consequent death toll, and add the confusion and controversy over immigration laws and practices and you'll see the manifestations of the root causes of our faltering democracy. Our two-party system, at both the Federal and State level is in partisan deadlock, and all of this resistance

----

* Compared to Donald Trump, Captain Bligh would appear to be a fairy godmother. Actually, Bligh may not have been the sadistic martinet popular representation has made him out to be. See *The Mutiny on Board H.M.S. Bounty* by William Bligh; Signet Books, 1961. There should be no such rational controversy regarding Trump.

and obstruction to sensible and just guidance is cloaked in the specious guise of individual human rights and civil liberty.

On the reverse of the Great Seal of the United States is inscribed *Annuit Coeptis* (He, God, has favored us). Well, on the belt buckle of a dead German soldier you would see *Gott Mit Uns* (God is With Us); but let's not go into the analogy. Could we come up with a new Latin motto such as *Novus Ordo Seclorum* (A New Order of the Ages)? To satisfy those who, having read "A New Order" and were taken aback by thoughts of Hitler's Nazism, we could alter that a little to *A New Democratic Order of the Ages*. Whatever we do, if we're even capable of getting out of this domestic mess we have permitted ourselves to wallow in, at least until we're on an even keel, is to put some teeth into those mealy-mouthed suggestions, advisories, and enticements and start telling people what they must do, or else. Or else there will be penalties. Must we wait until some unruly passenger on a commercial airliner causes it to crash, killing hundreds of people? Must we wait until Wall Street in its connivance with its lackeys in Washington finish turning us into a two-class society of haves and have nots, as in Lang's *Metropolis*? Must we wait until our children are the least (or worst) educated children in the world? Must we wait until the truckers have decided they've done enough damage to the supply chain, and consequently to boost inflation? Must we wait until the fossil fuel magnates have done their share to cause the record-breaking droughts and flood the streets of several Atlantic Seaboard cities? And not least, must we wait until more people are shot to death in this country than die in auto crashes, drug abuse, and cancer combined each year? It is Trump and his adherents who are trying to make what is strong "just," but it was we, the people, who have permitted the current state of affairs in which we find ourselves.

Here I must digress again, this time to make you *au courant* of recent events in our ineffectual, one could even say submissive battle with climate change. Several years ago a meteorologist aptly said that weather is a mood, but climate is a personality. Well described, but in this case that personality has changed from a usually tolerable, even amiable at times, and more or less predictable one to something closer to Victor Frankenstein's yellow-eyed, black-lipped fiend when he felt he had been unjustly and harshly dealt with and foiled in his attempts to be treated with understanding and even kindness. Finally, he gave up trying to be one with man and became the terrorizing creature we see him as today. He wanted friendship and understanding, but received abuse instead, and so became man's enemy.

The analogue is imprecise; it's difficult to bring something so abstract as Mother Nature to life, but the underlying idea of abuse and indifferences is basically the same. If we have become the recalcitrant, willful, and ungrateful children of a patient, though sometimes stern, mainly fair, and reasonably liberal provider we call Mother Nature, and have provoked her beyond endurance, she has given up on us and has become our enemy and a force to be reckoned with. In fact, the score on her side is rising increasingly to a point where I am having difficulty keeping track of her victories: one thousand houses totally destroyed by forest fires in Colorado; hundreds of vehicles stalled on Highway I-95 in Virginia for a distance of over forty miles because of unpreparedness for record-breaking snow and ice storms; "out of season," tornadoes and floods in Kentucky, Tennessee, and Arkansas that destroyed whole towns and killed scores of people; and in California, "America's Salad Bowl," a mere fraction of the snow pack needed to supply enough irrigation to provide for this year's crops, Lake Meade reduced to less than half its normal size, one third of our population enduring an unprecedented heatwave. All this, and we don't even know if Ol' Ma Nature has moved up her heavy artillery yet.

But it's time to get back on the road again, as Willy Nelson would say. Our fate is uncertain and unfortunately that is the only good news I have to give you. If we are to survive as a global species we won't find it out in astrological charts, or by reading the tea leaves in a cup, or by turning over Tarot Cards or reading the notes in Chinese fortune cookies. The only way we can have any assurance of our survival, however tenuous it may be, is by taking action, strong, positive action, now, before that potential enemy, Time, has sealed our fate.

21

Before my discussion on the progress of climate change I mentioned enlightened despotism. I suggested also that we retain that "enlightened," substitute "authoritarianism" for "despotism," and consider that as a possible way out of the potentially ruinous partisan maze we have gotten ourselves into. Our multiracial, multicultural populace with its countless religious persuasions would never tolerate a totalitarian form of governance, although in those desperate times of the Great Depression in the early 1930s serious consideration by some notable political observers and thinkers proposed that we try a form of fascism,* perhaps the syndicalism such as Mussolini instituted in Italy in the 1920s. Then came an interest in communism among people who now would be known as the Far Left. Many of them would come to regret that interest, and for some their engagement in that ideology when they came under the scrutiny of the McCarthy hearings in the early 1950s. But that merely is history; we must act now, from a position of strength as Pascal warned, to hold those responsible for the domestic chaos in which we exist and place Justice back on her rightful throne.

We could begin with the fulfillment of my greatest wish, which is that U.S. Marshals go to Donald Trump's palatial digs in Florida, frog-march him kicking and screaming into public view, put him in manacles and leg irons for all the

---

* For an extensive examination of fascism see *A Sharp Seasoning of Truth* by the same author.

world to see (on TV), and take him, not to some Club Fed, but to the Federal Detention Barracks at Leavenworth, Kansas and leave him to fend for himself among the general population there. To complete my wish, he would soon become aware that he was in the company of all his enablers and collaborators, to include those from Congress, other high Government officials, and others in the civilian sector who made possible his rise to and maintenance of such misbegotten power as has shaken this Democracy to its very roots.

Earlier I stated that our Constitution is not Holy Writ, as too many in and outside the Government prefer to see it.* Ironically, there are two billionaire oil barons in western Texas who agree but for an entirely different reason. Ferris Wilks (along with brother Dan), and Tim Dunn are quietly backing far right political candidates or punishing them by supporting their opponents. They too can see the Constitution's flaws, but in a totally different way than I. They would substitute it with the Bible. They even propose to replace public schools with "Christian" ones, a blatant abrogation of the separation of Church and State. Wittingly or not these Christian Nationalists are accessories to Trump's schemes for power, despite the fact that he isn't a Christian or knows what true and just nationalism is.

The Federal Government must begin to operate from a position of strength, not ruthlessly as did Hitler's Brown Shirts with their truncheons, or Mussolini's Black Shirts

---

* It was written by men, mainly well-intentioned young men, to provide guidance for a new democratic system of Government. Understandably, however well-meant, they could not foresee what the future of this new democracy would hold 220 years hence.

with their castor oil, but with appropriate authority and force to meet the situation. Reflect for a moment on the enforcement measures taken in response to that 1/6 attack on the Capitol. Instead of sending in piecemeal units of local police and dithering for hours about activating and committing National Guard troops, the Pentagon should have alerted the 82nd Airborne Strike Force at Fort Bragg, North Carolina and had them flown in from their adjacent Pope Air Force Base. While awaiting their arrival a few hours later, units of the D.C. and Maryland National Guard could have been called in to help the Capitol and Washington Metropolitan Police who were attempting, while hopelessly outnumbered, to quell the rioters. Upon their arrival that Strike Force would serve to "neutralize" the insurgent mob, using lethal force only in defense of their own lives, rounding up those who hadn't fled, and keeping them under close armed guard. Then with transportation provided by the National Guard units, the besiegers, who numbered over a thousand including those who may have escaped, should have been taken to an adequate holding facility, such as a sports stadium, and kept there under armed guard until a more appropriate holding area could be provided. There they would await judicial processing and final disposition. I stand by my suggestion that, so as not to overcrowd our Federal prisons, they all should be imprisoned at Guantanamo Bay until their sentences had been served. There it is: Justice, from a position of strength.

Elsewhere I have described in much more detail what form our system of democracy should take.* I call

---

* See "Renaissance" in *A Sharp Seasoning of Truth* by the same author.

it authoritative social democracy. Unfortunately too many uninformed Americans who hear the word "social" think of socialism, which they think of as being just a step away from communism.* Stupidity is merely an accident of birth; ignorance, especially about a matter of this seriousness is unforgiveable and even dangerous. But then, as Shakespeare's Puck said, "Lord, what fools these mortals be!"

There are those who suggest that we should form a third party. We can consider that when (and if) we get out of the mess we're in; we seem to be having enough trouble with two for the present.† What we must do is beat Trump's MAGA (Make America Great Again) at its own game. Trump's grandiloquent but deceptive motto has been used to mask his own megamaniacal and self-serving objectives of gaining absolute power in this country. We the people and victims of his attempted depredation of our democracy can do this by installing, for as long as it is needed, a system of enlightened authoritarianism to restabilize the chaotic state of the nation in which we find ourselves due to this unbalanced seeker of absolute power.

Confining those 1/6 rioters would have been a good step forward in my earlier suggestion that we winnow out

---

* We already have lost the use of "gay" in its original meaning, and "discrimination" has become problematical; "social" may follow "socialism" which already has become anathematized.

† Perhaps another "Independence" party, led by such present Senators as Angus King of Maine and Bernie Sanders of Vermont, and including Liz Cheney, Adam Kinzinger, Zoe Lofgren, and Adam Schiff, from the House of Representatives. An alternative name could be "Reform" party as failed Presidential Candidate Ross Perrot suggested thirty years ago. The latter name might be more suitable since it would be more descriptive of its *raison d'etre*.

the potential leaders of possible future similar events. I trust that the FBI and other law enforcement agencies continue and increase their efforts in finding, apprehending, and bringing the participants to justice.* But there is more to be done than just finding and apprehending those misguided and malintended "key communicators," as they are known in the field of psychological operations. We must ensure the loyalty of those we send to pursue them and upon whom we depend to defend and protect us. As I have pointed out, I'm speaking of our law enforcement agencies and our armed forces. At the siege of the Bastille in Paris in 1789 whole units of the King's troops joined the rebellious masses in the attack.

But there is more that we can and should do, and there will be many of you who will find the measures I will propose highly objectionable, or even outrageous. In speaking of an actual *coup d'état*, I stressed that in these times of advanced communications the extremists would know that control of TV and radio stations and not least the internet with its social networks, would be essential first objectives. We seem to be having difficulty in controlling the content of what comes and goes over those millions if not billions of internt exchanges that are carried *ad perpetuam*, night and day. Those op-ed pieces should come under the strict purview, screening, and censorship of the FCC (Federal Communications Commission), and if there are those who seek refuge in that First Amendment, we can remind them

---

* Of the 725 rioters found and charged in the Capitol raid, only 30 went to jail; and 70 were charged with misdemeanors, which Webster defines as "misdeeds." Eleven were charged with acts of conspiracy and sedition.

that free speech has its limitations, such as that venerable caveat so often used as an example: You can't shout "Fire!" in a crowded theatre, or use speech in inciting to riot, as did Trump on that fateful January 6th, 2021, with its attendant injuries and even deaths. Once again, if we're in a war, and I include the pandemic and the other crises I have described, why don't we stop talking and do something about it? And if we want peace and justice why won't we realize that we can only achieve those objectives from a position of strength? And who knows, perhaps when the emergency is over we may want to retain some of the adjustments we had to resort to when our very existence as a democracy was in danger of collapse.

We can't just tell others that we, as Americans, live in a democracy; we must prove it, even if we must remake it so, even if we must resort to the enlightened authoritarianism I have spoken of, in times such as these. As an essential part of this new departure we must stop suggesting, asking, even almost begging the public to do certain things, to take certain actions, and to avoid others, all for their own benefit, even to the point of saving their very lives. Getting vaccinated against this endless virus is just one prime example. In times such as these the Government must be in a position to mandate certain actions, or inactions, which can be just as important, or even vital. We can do this under a war powers act, but we must do so with caution, for power can be intoxicating.*

---

* As in the case of Huey Long when he was the Governor of Louisiana in the 1930s. Power can corrupt, as can its lack. A balance must be maintained between authority and freedom; as the Romans put it: *omnes deteriores sumus licentia* – too much freedom debases us.

The exercise of strength, or power, from above, requires planning and organization before any extensive operation is begun. For a nationwide campaign such as I envision, which would include details of logistics, personnel, and not least intelligence about any number of matters, a good deal of effort would be required. I can only hope that such an urgent and crucial effort would be made.

Many of you in what is left of our capitalist-driven democracy will find my next suggestion objectionable, as in certain other matters, and I'm sure that there are those of you who even will think it abhorrent. But it might be helpful here to recall what I've said about Wall Street, which continues to thrive despite all our problems, and Main Street, which is forced to bear the brunt of those problems. Remember also that the majority of those who can afford to invest in stocks and bonds don't need the profits they receive.

My suggestion is that we should nationalize a number of our corporations and other overgrown commercial entitles engaged in nationwide and in many cases global profit-making activities. The late President Reagan invoked such authority during the strike of our air traffic controllers, citing the public welfare as his motive. Some of the commercial enterprises or entities that should be considered for such an undertaking are: the commercial airlines; the pharmaceutical manufacturers; the firearms and ammunition companies; the railway and large trucking companies; the major oil producing and coal mining companies; the gas and electric power companies; the auto manufacturing companies; and the TV and internet moguls. Yes, drastic measures, for dire times.

22

Where do we begin, faced with such a herculean and daunting task? The first step would be to establish a suitable organization for planning and supervising the execution of the mission. The commission, of whatever it may be called, should be composed of representatives from the Departments of Commerce, Labor, Interior, Treasury, Transportation, Energy, Defense, and State, as well as a representative of the EPA (Environmental Protection Agency), with a chair person appointed by the President. Other representatives could be included if it were decided they were necessary, as well as those from the entities that are to be considered for nationalization, but only on an *ad hoc* basis. Alternatively, if one or more of the entities that I have suggested could convince the authorities, without specious inducements, that their inclusion would be nonproductive, or worse, counterproductive, they could be excluded.

One thing is certain: we must establish some sort of centralized agency to defend against cyber attacks. As matters stand now the targets of this extremely threatening, if more subtle type of warfare stand alone without any coordinated resources except those they can provide themselves on an individual basis. Witness that series of "ransom ware" extortions that continues throughout the country, such as that pipeline cut on the East Coast. Now try to imagine the state of this nation should our power grid(s) be rendered useless from coast to coast. Ask yourself, what does not operate on electrical power in this country today? Just follow yourself through the routine of a typical day in your life; now picture yourself doing everything in total darkness, at least for half of every day, not just for a few hours or days, but indefinitely. And even the best batteries don't last forever, and generators do run out of fuel.

In order to have any hope of success in such an ambitious and challenging endeavor as transforming our already fractured, unstable democracy into a reliable and just, and still democratic system of governance, another organization would be required in the interest of national security. This other group would be appointed by the President, with the recommendations of his advisors, and with the Secretary of Homeland Security as its Chairman. Other members of the organization would include but not be limited to: the Secretaries of Defense and Labor or their representatives, the Attorney General, Director of the FBI, Director of National Intelligence or their representatives, the Directors of Health and Human Services and Centers for Disease Control, one member from each political party in each house of Congress, and last but not least the Director of the Psychological Operations School at the JFKIMA (Institute for Military Assistance) at Fort Bragg, North Carolina.

Apropos of that last proposed member, presently Public Law 108 forbids the conduct of any propaganda targeting U.S. citizens. Under the Foreign Intelligence Surveillance Act (FISA) our counterintelligence can probe for foreign intelligence agents within the bounds of the United States. Those latter operations are carried out by the CIA, the

Department of Homeland Security, and the FBI,* which unfortunately has proven its ineptitude and blundering innumerable times. Ironically, we have been subjected to government and commercial propaganda since the earliest days of our independence. Former President Trump, wittingly or not, is conducting one of the most successful propaganda campaigns I've ever heard or read about, barring that of Joseph Goebbels under the Hitler regime, and it's highly likely that he has never heard of PL 108, that is restricting (legally) those of us who by now should realize that we are losing the fight to preserve our democratic way of life. We must fight fire with fire, as the old adage goes and as those heroic firefighters out West are trying to do, unavailingly I'm sorry to say. But we won't be fighting forest fires if we do as I have suggested, we'll be fighting another kind of incipient conflagration called an insurrection of nationwide proportions. We either migrate docilely to the sea and drown ourselves as do those lemmings annually in Norway, or we can confront the enemy squarely and defeat him, using some of his own tactics and strategies. And I will tell you once again, with metaphysical certitude, that in a propaganda campaign, changing people's attitudes is of little or no use without producing a change in their behavior, a change that will achieve your objective(s), and in our case, the Government must lead the way.†

---

* As in the case of Dr. Nassar and his young gymnast victims, the 9/11 and 1/6 catastrophes, or the standoff with David Koresh and his cultish adherents that ended so tragically, to cite merely a handful.

† And if that isn't true then I wasted my time as Director of Tactics at the Psychological Operations School for two years up there on "Smoke Bomb Hill" in the JFKIMA at Fort Bragg.

As for our intelligence resources, we need information about our domestic enemies as urgently as we ever needed it about our foreign threats. Here the words of the ancient Chinese sage, Sun Tzu, from his seminal work, *On the Art of War*, come to mind: "If you know the enemy and you know yourself, you need not fear the result of a hundred battles. If you know yourself but not the enemy, for every victory gained you will also suffer a defeat. If you know neither the enemy nor yourself, you will succumb in every battle." What we need now is that branch of intelligence the British call MI-5 and we know as counterintelligence, working in close coordination with the FBI to identify and detain those leaders and key communicators in that "winnowing" operation I described earlier. Such an operation must cover our entire societal spectrum, to include government officials and employees at every level and to include all members of the armed forces. With seventeen intelligence agencies harnessed to the task such a mission should not be unmanageable. With so many agencies engaged in intelligence gathering, even if their objectives are bound to be selective, there still would be a good deal of duplicative effort, but the task could be accomplished. This monumental effort would compel them, in close coordination with each other, to pursue a common goal (and, to some extent, justify their existence). So much for the altruistic but in this case self-defeating constraints on psychological and intelligence operations within the homeland.

More breaking news, on the lighter side for those of you I've wearied during our ramble by leading you through what John Bunyan might have called a slough of despond. But let me proceed with some of this lighter news. Following Britney Spears and Captain Kirk in their moments of fame,* and then news about those world-renowned tennis players, we now are being kept *au fait* with the riveting events surrounding Will Smith's assault on Chris Rock at the last Academy Awards presentations. But that was only equaled by the announcement that famed if philandering Tiger Woods (a blond, blue-eyed filly for every golf course, with another at home with the kids), recovering from a near fatal car crash, will compete in the Masters' Tournament this year. And incidentally, although Captain Kirk and giant phallic-shaped space vehicle have faded from the headline news, it recalled to me Victor Appleton's series of books about the adventures of boy hero Tom Swift, who showed what he could do around the time the Wright brothers invented the airplane. So his young fans had *Tom Swift and His Flying Machine.* Many years later, when I still was a boy I found *Tom Swift and His Giant Cannon* much more interesting than hearing about Captain Kirk and his giant whatever you wish to call it, today. We've all heard about the Mile-High Club, and although there may have been a woman aboard his spaceship, I don't think that Kirk, at the age

---

* I was gratified to see that our latest projectile to be shot into "space," however tentatively, looks more like a hypodermic needle than a human phallus. Whatever it may look like it already cost our taxpayers four billion dollars in its prelaunch cost, thus far just here on earth. Now, due to a serious hydrogen leak, it's "window" for launch has been indefinitely delayed and the prelaunch cost will continue to rise. Often I hear, "Well, anyway, it's at the Government's expense." Wrong. The Government has no money, except what they might collect in fines here and there; it's your money, the taxpayers, they are spending.

of ninety-one, would have been interested in establishing a Hundred Mile-High Club. In any case, if we don't go back to the swamp I won't be able to finish this rambling exposition.

23

Hindsight is, as some would say, 20-20 vision, and in our situation today it could be invaluable for our future. As that old aphorism tells us, if we ignore our past mistakes we will be bound to make them again in the future, or words to that effect. But we are making those same mistakes now, and no matter how dire the situation becomes we continue to make them. After more than three years of enduring the pandemic and no lessening of our other problems, we wish for a return to "normalcy" without doing what we must do to resolve them. Although I fervently wish it weren't so I have had to conclude that aside from the vicious political partisanship that is shaking our democracy to pieces, a dangerously large part of our populous is in some never-never land, much like children who won't face reality, and can't be made to understand that the world is, among many other things, not full of cotton candy, toy balloons, and trips to Disneyland. They must learn as they grow into adulthood that it isn't a world of dope, guns, pornography, "concerts," TV, and video games.* But then, with so many parents who haven't grown up themselves, who is there to teach them? We, as a nation, have become too adept at putting party hats on dung heaps.

-----

* Juvenal said that the Romans, once rulers of the known world, had come to care for nothing but handouts and spectacles, and *panem et circenses* (bread and circuses) was the favorite formula for Roman leaders who wanted to keep the allegiance of the masses. Some things change in name only; today we have Doritos, Superbowls, or other sport spectacles.

As I write, Ukraine is being reduced to ruins by every conceivable weapon in the Russian arsenal, with the exception (thus far) of the NBC (nuclear, biological, chemical) triad.* In the First World War Lewisite (mustard gas) and Adamsite (chlorine gas) were used by both sides in the conflict. These were outlawed by the Geneva Convention after the war. In the Second World War all sides used white phosphorous in all indirect fire weapons (howitzers, cannon, mortars, rocket launchers). Our 4.2 inch mortars were known as "chemical" mortars. I hope that white phosphorous has gone the way of those two horrible predecessors of the Great War, and is still not lurking in that valley of indecision we are pleased to refer to as "humane" ground warfare. White phosphorous, having made contact with the human body, burns its way through all tissue to the bone, and there is no way to stop it. If there is no international law preventing its use, the Russians could use it and escalate the terror they already

---

* The fact that a number of the largest corporations in the U.S. continued to do business in Russia during her ravaging of Ukraine only reaffirms what I've said repeatedly about our obsession with the acquisition of wealth. McDonald's, Burger King, Pepsicorp, and Chrysler Motors are among the profit seekers, with Pepsicola showing a profit of six and one-half billion dollars in Russian sales last year. A steel mill in Colorado, under an umbrella of other companies, owned by a Russian oligarch named Abromowitz, is still shipping steel to Russia thus helping, however indirectly, to kill Ukrainians. The rub being that if the mill were shut down some 1400 Americans would lose their jobs. This is analogous to the British munitions company that was still shipping their lethal products to Germany during the early stages of the Great War, when British troops in the trenches fighting alongside their French allies were being killed or wounded on the Western Front.

are subjecting the Ukrainians to. I hope I haven't erred in bringing this detail into the light.*

Over seven million Ukrainians have been displaced by the war; more than half that number have fled the country while the rest have been displaced internally. Thousands more are huddling under the rubble of their destroyed cities, towns, and villages. Those fleeing the country, almost all women, children, and old men, are attempting to go to the West, over hazardous routes, to cross into neighboring countries, mainly to Poland where they are being well treated. Eventually, however, Poland will begin to have problems of its own due to the massive and continued influx.

President Biden has announced that the U.S, will accept 100,000 Ukrainian refugees who are fleeing the Russian onslaught in their millions; a handsome gesture, relatively. Relatively because more than seven million Ukrainians, mainly women and children, already have fled into countries that surround their beleaguered homeland. Several million more have been displaced and are seeking refuge somehow somewhere in Ukraine itself. So Biden's seemingly generous offer of safe haven becomes somewhat pale by comparison when one considers that the cumulative population of those nations that are welcoming those displaced Ukrainians is roughly a third of ours.

I fully realize that we already are trying to resolve, clumsily and thus far unsuccessfully, problems of our own on our border with Mexico, with tens of thousands

____

* In fact, a recent news report has stated that the Russians, after having evacuated Snake Island, off Odesa in the Black Sea, have now bombarded it with white phosphorous.

of prospective, and desperate, refugees from south of the border seeking asylum here in the U.S. I realize also that there exists a geographical problem. Those Ukrainians who are being displaced are 4000 miles away from the western hemisphere, and three-quarters of that distance is open sea (or all 4000 miles if Ukraine still has access to the Black Sea). Still, a number of Ukrainians have appeared among those Hispanics on our southern border; somehow, they managed to get across to the Americas. I suggest that we could give some impetus to the President's offer by utilizing those C-17 cargo planes that are coming into Poland with arms and equipment to be transshipped into Ukraine. If they are not reloading with cargo or troops, or even if they are but with space still available, and are deadheading back to Dover, AFB or to somewhere else in the States, they could take hundreds of refugees with them. Those welcoming and praiseworthy Poles have taken in millions of those poor homeless people, but inevitably the strain on their administration, and even societally, may become too burdensome however willing they may be to handle the situation.

One of President Putin's main objectives in attacking Ukraine was to prevent her from joining NATO, or so he has alleged. Ukraine, which is roughly the size of Texas, and with a population of 44,000,000 people, probably has the best army in Europe, but nothing to compare with that of Russia's armed forces. If Ukraine had been a member of NATO, quite probably the West, and especially the United States in its current situation of domestic political disarray, would not be in its state of potentially catastrophic dilemma. Despite the disparity in armament and numbers, the Ukrainians have demonstrated a valiant and whole-souled resistance to preserve their independence and democratic way of life. But to continue to do this they need help, massive amounts of armaments, to include tanks and antitank weapons, aircraft and long range (S-300 type) antiaircraft missiles as well as the lower altitude Stinger missiles they have been receiving, and not least medical and food supplies and other humanitarian needs. There was a time, when the Russians were massing on Ukraine's borders, when, if we had accepted Ukraine as a member of NATO, the Russian invasion may have been avoided and negotiations begun in earnest; that may have worked then, but is too late for any such ploy now.*

There seems to be a growing consensus among Western observers that the Ukrainians, given the proper weapons in the quantity required, might be just able to drive the Russians out of their country, for which they are battling so courageously, one could almost say lovingly, to preserve. But the dilemma persists. In addition to providing the wherewithal of war in sufficient quantity we must invoke that sanction of sanctions that the Europeans are reluctant to discuss. More than forty-five percent of Russia's gas and oil exports go to Western Europe. Imposing that sanction, cutting off the greatest source of Russia's international income, could well bring President Putin to serious negotiations instead of the farcical meetings that have been conducted thus far. In

---

* Declaring Ukraine a member of NATO, as I suggested elsewhere, when Russian forces were encircling Ukraine such a risk might have been feasible, causing Putin's agreement to negotiate. Once he crossed Ukraine's border, however, we could well have precipitated a third world war.

the meantime and as I've suggested already, the matter of Aerial Domain under International Law should be looked into apropos of no fly zones and other matters concerning the skies over Ukraine. We have maritime laws, such as the three or twelve-mile limits, and it seems to me that in this modern age of air travel there are laws applicable to the space, for an undetermined distance (infinity) immediately beyond the terrestrial surface, which is held to fall under the jurisdiction of the State controlling the surface. You might discover that over the land within Ukraine's borders she has jurisdiction over the space above it. The dilemma that now exists for the U.S. and its NATO allies lies in the fear that the measures which I have suggested we take may lead to the escalation of this confrontation sufficient to induce the monomaniacal Putin to employ one or more of the unthinkable NBC weapons in his arsenal that he has already placed on standby. A *casus belli* that has the Allies stymied. We are between Scylla and Charybdis about what arms we can give to the gallant Ukrainians (jet fighter bombers, long range rockets, heavier artillery) without risking a third world war. And those Javelins we have been giving them require hundreds of semiconductors each and China was our main supplier. Added to our domestic problems is the fact that China, due to its restrictions in fighting its pandemic problems, no longer is sending us the constrast dyes needed to perform accurate readings of CAT and PET scans or MRIs.

Meanwhile, the Russians seem to have abandoned their attempts to occupy the Ukrainian capital of Kiev and are repositioning and resupplying their forces in the southeast, opposite that Donbas region, where all this *Sturm und Drang* began eight years ago, and the Ukrainians are moving to meet them there. The inevitable battle for or in the Donbas will be markedly different than the fighting we have been seeing in and around Ukrainian towns and cities. This will take place in relatively open terrain, what some would call "tank country," in which mechanized vehicles such as tanks, self-propelled artillery, armored personnel carriers, and tactical air support will be essential to its outcome. The weapons and ammunition the Ukrainians have been beseeching the West for could be crucial to that outcome.* A few elderly Russians or Germans, and all military historians could tell you about the Battle of Kursk, in Russia during WWII. Thousands of tanks were destroyed before the Russians could claim a Pyrrhic victory. Donbas, though it might be a Kursk in microcosm, if the Russians overcome those heroic Ukrainians may surpass it if only in the history books, as the Greek stand at Thermopylae has overshadowed so many other military encounters. Could President Zelensky, if only metaphorically, go down in history as a latter-day noncombatant Leonides?

---

* As Winston Churchill told FDR before we entered the Second World War, "Give us the tools, and we'll finish the job."

24

I have no idea if Putin's highly anticipated "false flag" operation as an excuse for invading Ukraine had any success or was even attempted; it has little or no meaning now. However, such a deceit on such a relatively small scale is not preserved for use only by an aggressive enemy. Yes, the ancient Greeks had their Trojan Horse, and as I've pointed out elsewhere Hitler had his specious excuses for invading Poland and the reacquisition of the Sudetenland. Perhaps most memorable was Hitler's desperate attempt to turn back those "Battling Bastards of Bastogne" (our 101st Airborne Division) in the Ardennes late in World War II by infiltrating our lines using German soldiers wearing U.S. uniforms, driving captured U.S. vehicles, and who spoke perfect "American" English.

But I can think of one example for the "friendly side" which, although fictional, will serve our purpose. During the Napoleonic Wars C.S. Forrester's naval hero, Horatio Hornblower, while cruising in the Bay of Biscay, learns the French secret signal that identifies their warships (both sides recommissioned and renamed captured enemy ships). Captain Hornblower, commanding a British frigate captured from the French and refitted, has the signal reproduced by his sailmaker and run up to his masthead. Thus he is permitted to enter a French naval base where four ships of the line (battleships) are moored side by side awaiting refitting for further duty at sea. As his frigate sails close-in to this unresisting, helpless flotilla, he delivers broadside after broadside into them, dismasting them and otherwise disabling them for further sea duty. All good fun, but unfortunately for Hornblower and his crew the French shore batteries had something to say to them on their way out.

As madcap a scheme as it may seem, I could suggest we take a leaf from Hornblower's logbook and refit a couple of vintage (diesel-powered) submarines, to lend some plausibility to the deceit, bearing identifiable Ukrainian insignia, get them into the Black Sea, and while Odessa (now Odesa) still is a viable Ukrainian port, torpedo and sink or disable every surface vessel the Russians have positioned in the area. These same submarines, should they survive such an escapade, could also serve, with all possible intelligence assistance from NATO, to intercept and delay or deny the progress or arrival of transports bringing Russian reinforcements from the Far East to fight in the Ukraine. A madcap scheme, perhaps, but so was Hannibal's crossing the Alps on elephants.

I can suggest another ploy that might allay fears of further escalation. Some of those long range (300 miles) rockets must have been duds. Back-engineer one or more Russian rockets, claiming the Ukrainians used the services of a defected Russian rocket expert to produce replicas, manufactured by the Ukrainians arms industry during the Russian incursion into the Donbas and its subsequent invasion of Ukraine in a secret arms factory (underground) near Kyiv. Then, using the counter battery radar we've provided them, locating Russian artillery and rocket launching positions inside the Russian borders, and with their Russian type rockets (long range) bearing Ukrainians ordnance markings, drive the Russians back. This is a war, and respect of borders should be meaningless. Did Hitler need permission to invade Poland in 1939, or to cross the French border a year later?

With President Putin rattling his nuclear sabre, we must be alive to the probability—the possibility has existed since 1945—of a nuclear war sometime in our future, assuming Mother Nature permits us to have a future. With the proliferation of nuclear weapons and their delivery means today the odds are in favor of this dismal prediction. What has come to be known as the "N" word may have a totally different and much more ominous connotation in the not so distant future. Putin's ambitions doubtless transcend his more immediate objectives to subjugate Ukraine; a brief look at the map of eastern Europe coupled with his recent pronouncements to the world at large about a "Russian Empire" will bear this out. There will always be "Putins" somewhere on the international stage, men in positions of power and authority to whom words such as independence, freedom, liberty, and especially democracy are meaningless. These are people for whom no action, no behavior, no stated ideology, however base, immoral, or criminal, is unjust and not to be tolerated; in a word, they are totally ruthless. As to Putin himself, and as I have asked elsewhere: if we have allowed a paranoid, narcissistic sociopath to occupy the White House for more than four years, why can't the Kremlin have its megalomaniac?

I know little about the Ukrainian Air Force. I don't know how many airplanes or pilots they have (or had).* Even if I had the quantitative knowledge I wouldn't know where they were located. Nonetheless, I could suggest those pilots man those planes and, hoping they wouldn't be intercepted by Russian planes or shot down by antiaircraft fire, cross the border into Poland. There they could be reorganized, reequipped, rearmed, and sent back to try to achieve that air superiority which, under existing circumstances, would be next to impossible since the Russians would be flying state-of-the-art aircraft and would outnumber them. We should keep in mind what I've said about aerial domain and the possible jurisdictional rights of the Ukrainians' airspace above their territorial boundaries under International Law. However infeasible such an endeavor might appear, it would not be a bad idea to organize and set in motion an evasion and escape plan for downed pilots who must be out there somewhere in what some would describe as the fog of war. Another madcap scheme, more in keeping with false flag operations, would involve re-marking a wing of fighter-bombers, perhaps those U.S. F-35s, touted to be the best of their kind in the world, with Ukrainian insignia, gathering volunteer pilots from all NATO nations, outfitted in Ukrainian flight suits, and send them to form an "aluminum umbrella" over Ukraine. The pilots could

---

* Quite probably, when the Soviet Union collapsed they were left with obsolescent MIGs and other earlier generation aircraft, both rotary and fixed wing, from the Soviet inventory, as was the case with other nations such as Poland, the Baltic states and others that had been subjugated by the USSR.

even be issued "L" pills (cyanide) in the event they were downed and captured alive.

The establishment of a no-fly zone over Ukraine, however it might be managed, though it might end the war or at least bring Putin to the negotiating table, would place the West on the horns of a seemingly insoluble dilemma. Although the people of Russia would be as opposed to another world war as those of virtually all other nations, under the iron hand of President Putin they have (as yet) no choice in the matter.* Without that no-fly zone the Ukrainians are literally begging for, hostilities will grind on, evolving into an oppressor-partisan conflict that the Russians could not win, but during which the Ukrainians would continue to lose thousands of innocent lives. As matters stand now and as is too often the case, only the war will win.

So the war will go on, and its end won't be made any sooner if our newscasts keep telling Putin's intelligence gatherers in detail the amounts and specific types of weapons and ammunition the U.S. and the rest of its NATO allies are sending the Ukrainians. As retired U.S. Army General Wesley Clark has wisely pointed out, "We should stop talking (publicly) about what we can do, thus telling Putin and giving him more reason to escalate the conflict, and just do it." Another example is a comment by Representative Andy Barr of the House Foreign Relations Committee about bringing in jet aircraft left in Poland,

---

* In ancient Rome, Putin's motto might have been: *Oderint Dum Metuant* (Let them hate, provided they fear), recalling Nixon's Chief of Staff, H.R. Haldeman, and the sign on the wall behind his desk with the dictum: Get Them By The Balls And Their Hearts And Minds Will Follow.

as were others in Soviet occupied countries after the fall of the Soviet Union, to be "backfilled" by newer aircraft from the U.S., while the obsolescent Soviet jets, piloted by Ukrainians, establish a no-fly zone over Ukraine. * Putin's actions speak loudly enough; we need give him no reason to react to ours. With Putin still in command, NATO's taking control of the skies over Ukraine, however it might be managed, inevitably would provide a *casus belli* for war between the West and Russia, and again, with Putin at the helm in the Kremlin, quite possibly a nuclear one.

I must admit it wasn't until I went through the Army's Nuclear Weapons Employment Course I learned that in the conduct of ground warfare, units at all levels that have sustained losses of ten percent or more in casualties are considered to have become ineffective or incapable of accomplishing their missions. I was made aware of this when I had to tally (estimate) casualties on both sides of a simulated conflict that involved the use of tactical nuclear weapons and the resultant massive casualties, despite the fact that the same percentage of casualties had already existed throughout the course of many non-nuclear wars. I was reminded of this when I heard a recent report that in this Ukrainian conflict the Russians had already suffered more than that ten percent in casualties, to include more than a dozen generals. With all their problems of logistics and ground operations in general, as with that now almost mythical forty-mile-long convoy early in the war as only

---

* They would find that the MIG-29 has come a long way since the days of the MIG-15s of Korean War memory when they were in aerial combat with our F-80 Shooting Stars and F-86 Saberjets. The same would apply to the Russian T-72 tank compared to the T-34's used in WWII and Korea.

one example, I'm almost convinced that Putin's army, at least as to their troops and their leaders, is as obsolescent as many of the weapons we no longer employ. So Putin has been driven to bombarding Ukraine out of existence with rockets, artillery, and air strikes.

I recall the Red Army of WWII that some referred to as "The Russian Steamroller," whose leaders* considered artillery "the god of war." When the course of the war was reversed at the Battle of Stalingrad, they demonstrated that belief during a formidable engagement on an extended front when the Russians stopped the Germans by employing what they called "hurricane fire," lining up their artillery pieces of all calibers, hub-to-hub, and delivering barrages and concentrations until the enemy was turned back. At Stalingrad, incidentally, the Russian infantry fought as stubbornly and courageously as the Ukrainians are fighting today, and they were victorious and changed the course of that war.

I can't tell you much, if anything, about the current state of Russia's armed forces, military, naval, or air, since I've been out of the "need to know club" for many years now. I can tell you that if we were to conduct an inventory and readiness inspection of what's in those silos out West in the U.S. and at locations near certain air bases and naval installations here and abroad, we would find that the Russians have inherited as many or more nuclear weapons and their delivery systems from the Soviet regime as we have in our inventory. I can tell you also that the nuclear proliferation in nine other nations

---

* Those high-ranking officers who had survived Stalin's purge in 1937, driven by his paranoid distrust of their loyalty.

that are not considered allies or friends of ours continues. The fact that North Korea and Israel are leading the way in nuclear weapons development should be of interest to you also, as is the fact that neither of those two countries voted in the U.N.'s General Assembly to remove Russia from the United Nations Council on Human Rights.*

What I do know is that we've got at least a dozen aircraft carriers with an untold number of aircraft aboard, surface warships and submarines armed with both conventional and nuclear weapons, an Air Force with heavy bombers, fighter-bombers, and fighters, troop and cargo planes, air-to-air tanker refuelers, Cruise missiles and their naval counterparts, Tomahawks, air-to-air, ground-to-air, and ground-to-ground missiles to compete with those of any potential enemy. Although by percentage we have more combat tested soldiers, we may fall short in overall numbers (especially with 24 veterans committing suicide daily), which may require, however reluctantly, the reinstitution of conscripted service if we go to war with Russia. The assets I have listed, and some I have not, are located at 700 bases throughout the world. For some, this may come as reassuring news; for the general public it may help to explain why our annual defense budget is nearing a trillion dollars.

If Putin, whose most cherished desire is to go down in the history books as Vladymir the Great, initiated a war

---

* The U.N., like its predecessor the League of Nations is based upon man's innate goodness and his love for his fellow man, neither of which exist. Instead of cleaving to this hopeless, altruistic nonsense it should have an armed force behind it such as does NATO. Was that League of Nations able to prevent the Second World War? And Russia still has a seat on its Security Council as does China.

with NATO, as he has intimated in his veiled threats and actions, he might do so using nuclear weapons, and if so, they probably would be the relatively lower yield tactical weapons of the battlefield.* If instead he chose to employ strategic city or installation destroying weapons from the outset of hostilities, we and the rest of the world might avoid the now seemingly inevitable fate that Good Old Mother Nature has in store for us. As it is we now are receiving reports that the Russians may employ chemical or even biological weapons in this present conflict in which we are getting more and more involved.

As I leave this somber subject and move toward the end of this dissertation I would like to pose a question for your consideration about the situation I have just described: What do you suppose President Putin would have done if NATO, with the full approval of the European Union, were to have invited and accepted, *ex post facto*, Ukraine as its thirty-first member, when his forces were positioning themselves on Ukraine's borders but had not crossed them yet, accepted Ukraine with full benefits, including that Fifth Article of the NATO Pact: war with one means war with all?

---

* As early as the 1950s, during the height of the Cold War, we had types of tactical nuclear weapons to be delivered by such now obsolete systems as our old Honest John rocket launcher, our eight-inch howitzer, one of the most accurate artillery pieces ever produced, which might still be in service, and our massive 280mm "atomic cannon" that in its relocations throughout what then was West Germany ruined a number of beautiful structures, both archaic and restored, after Allied bombings during WWII. There also was a SADM (small atomic demolition munition). This implosion-type device would fit in a bowling ball bag, and I sometimes wonder why it or some similar device hasn't been used in today's "terror" attacks.

Lastly, apropos of matters nuclear, is the question of Chernobyl, which to some extent has been upstaged by the war itself. Natural hazards, droughts, tsunamis, and impacts from such extraterrestrial objects as meteors or asteroids, become natural disasters depending on geography, topography, and demography. A classic example was the asteroid impact in the vicinity of Tungusta, a sparsely inhabited area in Siberia in 1908. Vast areas of forest were destroyed, literally flattened, but few people were killed or injured. If that asteroid had torn into New York City, a million or more people would have been killed. The eruption of Mount Tambora in 1815, the most destructive explosion on earth, in present day Indonesia on the island of Sumbawa; which again, was sparsely populated two centuries ago, is another example.

Today, in the nuclear age, we have created a hazard of our very own; call it an unnatural hazard if you will, but it could result in disasters that would transcend our visions of Armageddon, though if administered properly could be a benefit to all mankind. Nuclear power is a two-edged sword, which showed its potentially disastrous side not merely at Hiroshima and Nagasaki, but at Three Mile Island in 1979, at Chernobyl in 1986, and at Fukushima in 2011. I've listed those calamities chronologically, but based upon those qualifying factors I've stated, Chernobyl leads the others in the magnitude of disaster at the time of the event and even, potentially, now. When the Russians occupied the place in late February and early March, 2022, they dug trenches and foxholes in what is called the Red Forest, an area still permeated with radioactivity. Those soldiers, if still alive, are ridden with radioactive poisoning from those persistent gamma rays in the soil. After the Ukrainians reoccupied Chernobyl scientists with dosimeters and Geiger counters recorded radiological levels fifty times higher than what is considered safe without protective clothing and equipment. Nuclear power can be a boon to us all, but we must keep in mind that other edge of its sword.*

---

* Now potential disaster looms again as the Russians are shelling and rocketing the largest nuclear power plant in Europe, at Zaporizhzhia, in Southern Ukraine. Having gained access to the plant itself they have begun firing at the Ukrainians from positions there, making it too dangerous for the Ukrainians to employ counter-battery fire. One can only hope that the U.N.'s IAEA (International Atomic Energy Agency) personnel who now are on the scene can bring some resolution to this potentially catastrophic situation.

25

On Independence Day, 2022, forty-two million Americans drove their cars fifty miles or more to celebrate the holiday somewhere other than at their own homes, despite uncommonly high gas prices at the pump. Fireworks were held in cities and towns from coast-to-coast, while rock bands and singers entertained multitudes of people. Yes, the entire country was celebrating. But, celebrating what? Aside from an allusion or two to that day almost 250 years ago when we declared our independence from England one wonders what we had to celebrate. As if to temper all this jubilation another kind of fireworks occurred at Highland Park, a suburb of Chicago, where a mass murderer shot seven people to death and wounded more than two dozen more during a celebratory parade there. So common an event did nothing to impinge on the festivities elsewhere. Would that more of us demanded that something substantive were done about gun violence rather than "pain at the pump" and elsewhere, or spiraling inflation in general while forty-two million Americans senselessly must drive themselves somewhere. Of course, it's all about money again, and that principle of economics called supply and demand is a major factor in the case of inflation. Purveyors of goods and services stay in business by making profits. When supply lags behind demand and they must sell or provide less in services, they must charge more to maintain their profit margin. And this takes me to what I want to say about what inflation can be like.

The first time I heard the word "inflation" used in an economics context and not having anything to do with proper pressure in my bike tires or a football (13 psi) was at the dinner table one evening when I was about twelve years of age. My aunt, who had married a German, born and bred, and her husband were there. When the Great War ended in an armistice, he was a teenager preparing to be conscripted into the German army. His father was killed in the battle for Verdun in 1916.

In those early days of World War II and the latter part of the Great Depression when everything seemed to cost a nickel, most Americans didn't even know what the word inflation meant; after all, the study of economics is still known as "the dismal science." In this case as it was during that failed period of Prohibition and it is with drug addiction today, inflation is mainly a matter of supply and demand, one of the first laws of Economics.

The British, abetted by the French, and ignored by the indifference of the Americans, imposed a naval blockade on the Baltic ports of Germany which lasted almost a year after the Armistice in 1918. Under the rapacious terms of the Treaty of Versailles the Germans were required to pay financial reparations so outrageously high it was impossible to meet them. The Allies confiscated all of Germany's warships and even the dirigibles that had bombed, however sporadically, England.* With all this, coupled with that

---

* Because my family lived only fifteen miles from Lakehurst Naval Air Station (where the Hindenberg disaster occurred) I was taken to see one of those behemoths, now renamed the Los Angeles and in commercial service, and to actually enter the passenger "car" with its red plush seats. It was an impressive experience for an eight-year-old-boy.

naval blockade, Germany was on her knees, with a great number of people literally starving. A German butcher in Hamburg was discovered to be abducting children of tender age, slaughtering them, cooking, canning, and selling the meat as pork. That German uncle of mine told us on that evening of long ago about his mother going to the market with a small wheelbarrow full of Deutsche Marks tied up in bundles and coming home with a loaf of bread, a head of cabbage, and a little butter. Many years later, when I was living in a sublet apartment in Heidelberg, there was a framed two-billion Mark note on the wall in the kitchen. Vindictive reparations, like unwise sanctions, can have disastrous results.* In this case they gave rise to Hitler, the Nazi regime, and a second world war. It didn't help that while so many Germans were suffering and literally starving to death, Josephine Baker, wearing nothing but a string of pearls, danced for rich German war profiteers (many of whom were Jewish financiers) in their homes or in cabarets on Berlin's Kurfurstendam.

Earlier I spoke of lemmings, those furry-footed arctic rodents whose migrations continue into the sea where vast numbers of them are drowned. I used those self-destructive little creatures as an allegorical metaphor to illustrate our own semi-suicidal predilection for the disintegration of our

---

* Currently, a year after our disgraceful departure from Afghanistan, leaving almost 80,000 of our friendly Afghan interpreters, translators, and other aides to their fate at the hands of the vengeful Taliban, and now they and the general populace are beginning to starve to death due to their failed economy, we are holding seven billion dollars of their capital assets to keep it from the Taliban. Of interest also is the fact that our twenty-year occupation of Afghanistan cost us two trillion dollars and almost 3,000 American lives.

unity and our democratic system of governance. That having been made clear, let us ascend now to avian creatures, to the eagle, and more specifically the bald eagle that appears on one side of the Great Seal of the United States of America and is the proud symbol of our Republic. Let us think carefully and honestly about that Great Seal that is affixed to all proclamations, ratifications of treaties, and certain instruments of international relations. Now let us think of our domestic turmoil and disunity. Does that proud eagle, with the olive branch of peace clutched in his right talons and the arrows of war in his left,* truly symbolize our state of unity in justice? What has fate in store for that proud (today some would say "haughty" or "arrogant") symbol of our Republic? That is what the people of this country must decide and act upon. For my part I hope fervently that it is not the tragic fate that the poet Byron described poetically two centuries ago:

> 'Twas thine own genius gave the final
> > blow,
> And help'd to plant the wound that
> > laid thee low:
> So the struck eagle, stretch'd upon the
> > plain,
> No more through rolling clouds to soar
> > again,
> View'd his own feather on the fatal
> > dart,

---

* Over the entrance to the centuries-old Armory in Venice is this dictum from Vegetius: *Qui Desiderat Pacem, Praeparet Bellum* (Let Him Who Desires Peace Prepare For War).

And wing'd the shaft that quiver'd in
     his heart.
And it was the wise and entertaining Aesop who told us two
and one-half millennia ago: "We often give our enemies the
means of our own destruction."
Finis coronat opus

www.ingramcontent.com/pod-product-compliance
Lightning Source LLC
Chambersburg PA
CBHW051442250726
48655CB00001B/197